THE VOW

———

TED BORN'S
LAST TRIAL

First Printing 2021

ISBN Paperback   978-1-7357825-6-0
ISBN Hardback   978-1-7357825-5-3

PREFACE

This is the second of a series of "Ted Born" novels involving a fictitious lawyer who happens to attract very challenging lawsuits, a sequel to the other recently released Ted Born novel, "The Impossible Mock Orange Trial," this time set some fifteen years later than the events of that first release. Ted finds himself a defendant against claims that could ruin him financially and destroy his personal and professional reputation, involving his succeeding the deceased brother of his impaired but wealthy client as manager of the client's affairs. A judge who seems likely to preside over the upcoming trial seems skeptical of Born's position, and possibly hostile. To complicate matters further, Born's own law firm, and his Firm's malpractice insurance carrier, are unhappy with this messy situation and want Born to get out of the case. With the client's family seemingly united against Born, his own law firm pressuring him to get out of the case, and facing a trial before an unfavorable judge, Born has to decide what course to take in accordance with his own values and ethics. This case raises questions about professional responsibility and basic right and wrong in the context of the vulnerable population of older persons whose longstanding estate planning efforts are in jeopardy due to members of their own families who are intent on scuttling the wishes and plans of the testator and substituting their own ideas.

In this case, Born had promised a wealthy philanthropist client, Alexander Carr, at the client's request and as an accommodation to him, that Born would serve as an alternate attorney-in-fact, trustee and executor in the event of death or incapacity of Carr's first-choice brother, John, *and* Born promised he would make sure that another brother, Jesse, estranged from Alexander Carr, would never get his hands on Alexander's finances.

Years later, the favored brother John dies unexpectedly at a time when the philanthropist is declining mentally and physically and Born is thrust into the position of being the primary manager of the assets of his philanthropic client under the long-standing estate documents of Alexander Carr. This new status for Ted Born is met with resistance by other family members and potential heirs of Mr. Carr, who contend that a family member should be in Ted's position as custodian of the wealthy man's assets. To squeeze Ted out of his position, estranged brother Jesse postures himself as Carr's "new best friend" and procures from him a superseding power of attorney that would enable him to undo his own brother Alexander's carefully constructed estate plans.

Vicious litigation follows, in which Ted is accused of having maneuvered himself into his position in order to get a big fee, breaching his fiduciary duty to his client Mr. Carr and interfering with the "new" power of attorney the estranged brother has procured. Ted finds himself trying to defend the long-standing instructions of his client, in the face of a putative new power of attorney replacing him with the estranged brother, signed by his own client – the issue being whether Mr. Carr knowingly and willingly had a change or mind or whether the estranged brother, with support of some other family members, took advantage of the mental and physical decline of the philanthropist to get a replacement document signed favoring Jesse and excluding Born.

This book contrasts the desires of an individual testator with desires of his family, and a lawyer caught in the middle, trying to uphold his own professional responsibilities at a time when he feels he is standing alone, with no real allies. It is intended to be a gripping story laying open a wide range of human emotions and motivations, with thoughtful content. This novel, like its predecessor, "The Impossible Mock Orange Trial," explores the ultimate question: "What is justice?" None of the characters represent any real persons, living or dead. It is a fiction novel but inspired in part by experiences of the author in his practice of law.

CHAPTER ONE

THE BIRTHDAY PARTY

Ted and Lydia Born were preparing to go to the social event of the year in Greenville. It was the 90th birthday party celebration of the wealthy philanthropist Alexander Carr, whose parties were the stuff of legends. It was of course a white tie formal affair, and Ted had a set of tails in readiness, which he occasionally needed for such occasions. The invitation list included mainly the upper crust of society, a list Ted and Lydia would probably fall short of, but they made the cut because of Ted's status as Alexander's lawyer. The Borns were glad to be invited, but they knew Alexander would be surrounded by large crowds of the local glitterati, and they would greet and speak with Alexander and then quietly be observers and peripheral participants in the festivities.

Ted had known Alexander for more than twenty years, beginning with a tax case he won for Mr. Carr, and from there he had handled whatever other legal matters the gentleman had - a lawsuit or two, but mainly Mr. Carr's wills and estate planning, of which there was plenty, considering his wealth and his continued refining of its ultimate disposition. Ted always called him "Mr. Carr" because he was twenty-some-odd years older than Ted, and he felt he owed his client that deference. For the client's part, he had never asked Ted to cut out the formalities and just call him "Zander," as his family and a few close friends called him. His considerable wealth and philanthropy earned him the attention and respect of many bigwigs who regularly solicited funds from him for their pet charity projects. He was intelligent, had strong opinions, and everyone listened when he spoke. He was always in charge.

Zander had been married, but his wife had passed away some years earlier, leaving him with four adult children. He had never remarried, although he had often remarked to close friends, with a grin, "The single lifestyle is tough, but the worst part of it is that the women won't leave me alone!" He was a handsome man, but his money could possibly have had something to do with his attractiveness.

Ted had never discussed with Mr. Carr the earlier stages of his life, as he felt it was none of his business. The closest the gentleman came to mentioning it was when he came to dinner at Ted and Lydia's home, a few years after his wife had left him a widower. It was a couple of weeks before Christmas, and the Borns' home had been all decorated with a big Christmas tree, and creches, and a lighted Dickens Village, along with lots of angels and Santa Clauses here and there. Christmas music was playing in the background on the stereo, and Lydia had prepared a beautiful dinner with salmon and vegetables, to be followed by Lydia's much-coveted charlotte russe for dessert. Mr. Carr was obviously enjoying the occasion, joining in several glasses of wine, commenting on the beauty of the Borns' young daughter Rebecca, and inviting her to come see his late wife's collection of dolls from around the world. And then the eyes of the guest began to show some slight tears, and he volunteered how much he felt the loss of his wife and of a family setting around Christmas, though remarking that his children were good about inviting him to their Christmas parties, some of which were at the Club or restaurants, not always in a home setting. Ted scarcely knew what to say. He mumbled something about the many friends Mr. Carr had and how many people loved and respected him, and the mood of the evening began to recover. It had been a bit awkward, but Ted knew Mr. Carr appreciated being asked to come over for dinner. It had been the only time in their entire relationship that he ever saw the austere Mr. Carr lose his composure. Generally, he was the stern CEO-type.

In the course of Ted's representation of Mr. Carr, he came to learn things about the state of his relationship to members of his immediate and extended family: two younger brothers - a bother John, married but without children, and another brother, Jesse, a bachelor until he married late in life, from whom he had long been estranged, all of which had figured into his estate planning. Mr. Carr deeply loved his own four children - three boys and a girl. His daughter Kate was the youngest of them, and she was obviously very special to Mr. Carr, although he carefully never articulated that.

Over the years, Mr. Carr had asked Ted to prepare a total of some twelve wills, as well as multiple codicils to each will, and Ted came to understand something of what it must be like to have a lot of wealth and no real, genuine friends other than his own children and one favorite brother John, a soulmate to whom he could relate – a success financially and socially, although not quite on the scale of Mr. Carr.

Ted and Lydia drove to the Club for the big birthday bash, gave the valet the car keys and found themselves in a long line of invited guests waiting to be received by the honoree. Upon entering the large Club living room, they noticed, and nodded knowingly to each other, the dominant red décor all around, reflecting Mr. Carr's favorite color. He felt that a bright red tone was suggestive of truth and certitude, hallmarks of his own values. So red roses and red carnations seemed to be everywhere.

Mr. Carr was seated in a tapestry-covered wing-back chair in the Club living room, surrounded by guests. Ted noticed that he sometimes squinted his eyes at the guests, a result of the progressive macular degeneration that had impaired his vision in recent years, rendering him almost functionally blind. He was attired in the obligatory white tie and tails, except in his case the bow tie was red and he wore a fresh red carnation in his lapel. This was his big night. His brother John was standing near him in the receiving line, also greeting guests with the honoree. Ted had come to know John a few years earlier as John began to assist his somewhat older brother increasingly in dealing with his home staff and financial matters. Most importantly, John had been much involved when Mr. Carr had set up a living trust to hold the bulk of his assets, to minimize the role of the probate process after death.

Ted noticed that brother Jesse and his wife were over in a corner of the room, mostly staying to themselves. When Ted and Lydia reached Mr. Carr in the reception line, Ted leaned over and grasped his hand, and the Borns wished him a happy birthday and complimented the magnificent floral arrangements all around   He did not need to introduce himself, as Mr. Carr could recognize voices of those in regular contact with him, a compensation for his diminishing eyesight. Ted noticed that the studs in Mr. Carr's shirt were real diamonds.

At the appointed time, a tuxedoed waiter with a hand-held xylophone entered the room and played a few bars to signify that it was time to move into the large ballroom, where the white linen-cover dinner tables, with red runners, were ready for guests, and where the orchestra, imported for the occasion, was playing background music. Mr. Carr led the way for the glittering elite group, sometimes grasping the arm of brother John and one of his sons who walked on each side of him. Mr. Carr was of course seated at the honoree's table, including, among other notables, the President of the University, a woman about 62 years of age, wearing an elegant diamond necklace.

At each table, there was a tall and gorgeous red-dominant flower arrangement, sparkling crystal figurines, as well as individually wrapped favors behind guest place cards. Brother John proposed a toast to Zander's health, with a wish for many more happy birthdays, to which the guests all joined with their pre-poured wine glasses. This was followed by toasts offered by the three sons and the daughter. Brother Jesse sat quietly through it all, but politely lifted his glass. The entrée was beef tenderloin with bearnaise sauce, accompanied by a medley of vegetables, and the dessert was chocolate roulage. There was of course an open bar, and, in addition, wine was served at the tables. In addition to the lovely desserts served at the tables, there was also a giant birthday cake brought in and put in front of the honoree for a symbolic moment and then available on a central table during the dance phase of the evening, for other guests to sample if they wished. Zander was able to rise from his table and thank the guests and then attempt a few dance steps with his University President table companion before taking his seat again for the remainder of the evening, while guests danced. The crowd in the dining room gradually dispersed as the evening wore on, thanking Mr. Carr and reiterating happy birthday wishes to him.

Ted and Lydia joined the other guests in individually thanking Mr. Carr for a wonderful evening, and then they made their way to the massive porte-cochere where the valet brought their car up. As they drove home, Ted mused, "Lydia, I just could not help but think of the contrast between the Mr. Carr I have known all these years and the one we saw tonight. Of course, it was a lovely party, and I am glad it could serve as a celebration of his life – and I hope he enjoyed it. But it pains me to see how far this grand and commanding man is sliding. Of course, I realize he is ninety years old, which is what this party was all about, but he has always seemed a pillar of strength. I somehow expected he would never change. I wish him many more happy birthdays, but I wonder about his ability to keep functioning. You know, I am his alternate Trustee and Executor if he should be incapacitated or pass away, and I would hold his power of attorney."

"I had almost forgotten about that, Ted," Lydia replied, to which Ted responded, "Well, you know, Lydia, I haven't talked much about it, but years ago when I was writing a will for him, I said, 'Mr. Carr, you have named your brother John as your executor, but you need to have a backup for him, as an alternate, in case he predeceases you.' He thought about it and said, 'Yes, I suppose I should have an alternate, but who? It can't be Jesse, because I don't want him EVER to have anything to do with my financial affairs. He mismanaged his own money, and besides that, we don't think alike and, frankly, we don't communicate with each other because of some bad incidents we've had. As for my children, I am not comfortable naming one of them. For one thing, I don't want to have to choose just one of them, nor do I want any one of them to have control relative to the others. My accountant is too old; I'll probably outlive him. Let me think about it and I will call you back.' In a few days he called me back and asked if I would serve as his alternate. He said he trusted my judgment and my integrity, knew the difficult obstacles I had overcome in my life, and felt I could handle everything properly and fairly. I probed as to whether there wasn't another person he could appoint. He said no one else he knew would be suitable.

"I was taken aback, because it had never occurred to me that I would be in the picture, nor had I desired to be. I thought about his request, and I finally agreed to do it as an accommodation, thinking it was highly unlikely that I would ever need to serve, and it enabled me to complete the work on his will that had been held up for that decision. Mr. Carr appeared to be in good health at the time, and his brother John was two or three years younger than he and was apparently in good health, plus, I thought, Mr. Carr might well change his mind in coming years, and it would all end up as a moot question. So, I did it as a formality, just so there would be *someone* named as a successor executor in the unlikely event that his brother John predeceased him. It still remains a formality in my mind as of today, because his brother John is still alive and seems to be in good health, but, seeing Mr. Carr tonight, I just began to think about it."

"And he kept you as his alternate during all these years, and all those new wills I've heard you mention, never changing that part of the wills?" Lydia asked rhetorically. "No, we've been through 12 different wills and probably 20 total codicils, one or two or more for every will," Ted reflected, "and he always said he wanted me as his alternate. In fact, just a few years ago, as we set up a living trust for him, in addition to having his will in place, he asked me specifically to be his alternate trustee under that trust. At the same time, on virtually every occasion a new will or a new codicil came up and we talked about the primary and alternate executors or trustees, he not only said he wanted me to stay as his alternate, but invariably added, 'I want you to understand that under *no* circumstance is Jesse ever to have anything to do with my estate or financial affairs. Do you understand that?' I would say, 'Yes, Mr. Carr, I completely understand your feelings about that, and I assure you that I will not ever let Jesse have anything to do with your financial affairs, if I ever have anything to do with it – although I don't think it will ever come up.' Then he looked at me and said, 'Do you swear to it?' I smiled and said, 'Yes, Mr. Carr, I swear to it. It is a solemn vow.' I was halfway joking, because I was amused with his concern about an unlikely, far-in-the-future, hypothetical event, but he did not smile. He took it dead seriously, I could tell. That was the first time."

Ted continued, "In all the subsequent meetings with him over the years, he would reinforce again that he did not want Jesse to have anything to do with his finances, and I would say, 'Yes, Mr. Carr, I've taken a vow to that. I won't let it happen if I can possibly avoid it. Rest assured.' He was obsessed with the fear that his estranged brother would ever get control of or get into his assets. And I gave him my regular assurance I would not allow it. But now, since he has begun to accumulate health problems, it is not just a hypothetical. I understand that, in addition to the macular degeneration in his eyesight, he either has diabetes or pre-diabetes, and bad arthritis, and God only knows what else. I'm not privy to his health records, and all I know is bits and slips he makes in conversation, like taking this or that medicine or that he has an appointment with such-and-such a kind of doctor, plus my own observation of his difficulty seeing and even signing his name. But being with him tonight, I just have to wonder what and when something could happen to him. Of course, his brother John is still there to step in and carry the ball, and I guess everything is all right for now."

"Well, let's just hope he has a long and happy life. Modern medicine can do a lot, and you've told me he has a fine concierge doctor looking after him. As you say, John is still available and seems very capable," Lydia said.

They pulled into their garage, greeted their dog, and then went to bed. It had been a long day.

CHAPTER TWO

A CHANGE IN THE WILL

"Hi, Ted, this is John Carr. I hope this is a good time to talk for a few minutes," Ted heard as he picked up his office phone. "Yes, John. Always a pleasure to speak with you. What can I do for you?" Ted asked. Although he still called Alexander "Mr. Carr," he had started out calling the slightly younger brother by his first name, which seemed all right, since Ted had put on a few years himself since first meeting Zander. It seemed natural to him, and John had never objected. Yet, Ted was aware that John was not just a brother to Mr. Carr. He was literally also, like his older brother, a "Who's Who" among local leaders of business, charities, and social affairs, reinforced by his wife Angela, who had a very long list of civic contributions and accomplishments in her own right. Notwithstanding their community status, John and Angela were very down-to-earth and never, ever, bragged about or even mentioned their accomplishments and honors - nice, solid people.

"It's about Zander's will. Now that I am taking over more responsibility to help him with his affairs, I have been reviewing the will, along with other things, and I noticed that it provides that his son Bruce is to inherit Zander's house. As you must know, the house has appreciated in value so much that it is going to result in a disproportionate inheritance for Bruce compared with the others. I thought that ought to be changed, and Zander agrees," John explained.

"I guess that would be true insofar as most of his children are concerned, but of course he also has provided for a special legacy gift to his daughter Kate – his widow's six-carat diamond ring - which also would seem to disproportionately favor her. Am I right?" Ted responded.

"You are correct about that, but somehow that seems all right to me because the ring should go to a female, and she is his only daughter, and the baby of the family. But the house is another matter, and I think we ought to equalize a little more in that case," John explained. "Okay, I can see that," Ted said, "and I understand Mr. Carr agrees. The obvious way to handle that issue is just to let the house be a part of the residuary estate, and it could be sold, and the proceeds put in the pot with all the other parts of the residuary estate, and then divided equally. I don't have the last will right in front of me just now, but I do remember that there is a whole laundry list of specific bequests, which might make the distribution a bit uneven, but I guess they are relatively small in the overall picture, and they don't bother you, I gather."

"No, they don't," John replied. "There are some nice items in those designated bequests, but they tend to even out and I don't think we need to worry about that. I would just make that one change with the disposition of the house. Now we might have a problem with Bruce, because Zander promised Bruce he would leave the house to him, and I think Bruce has been counting on it – including his wife. They might think this is a betrayal. But I think it's the right thing to do, and I think Bruce will get over it."

"Well, that's a family relations issue for you and Zander to handle," Ted mused. "As far as I am involved, if you and Mr. Carr tell me this is what he wants done, then I've got my marching orders, and we will do it. Circumstances change and it's Mr. Carr's property. He can do with it however he sees fit. I'll make a codicil to that effect, or maybe we will just make another new will. With computers, it's just as easy to do a new will as to add a codicil, and it has the advantage that all dispositions are covered in a single document. Anything else that needs changing?"

"I don't think so. You know you are the alternate trustee and the alternate executor. I hope you don't ever have to play those roles, because I hope I will be around for a while and can handle whatever is needed. But you know, Zander has a whole lot of confidence in you, and I think it is the right call, because I don't see any of his children doing that. For one thing, it could cause some friction, or even in-fighting, sort of putting one of his children over the others. Also, I've been impressed with your attention and obvious care for Zander's welfare. Needless to say, Jesse is not an option. But I do think Zander is beginning to really need help, and increasingly so. The other day I found that one of his sitters - he has 'round-the-clock sitters now, you know - had gotten hold of his checkbook and had forged his signature to pay the sitter's utility bill. I discovered it almost accidentally, and now that sitter is long-gone, but with Zander's progressive macular degeneration and health problems, he's vulnerable. I am afraid he is slipping somewhat mentally also - just little things now, but we need to watch it."

"John, do you think he has a competency problem? If he does, he can't make a valid new will, and the issue about the disposition of the house would be a moot question," Ted said with a slight frown on his face.

"Ted, I don't think it has gotten that bad yet," John assured him. "But he's 91 years old, and I began noticing small problems, well, really about the time we were planning his 90th birthday celebration, and in the last year or

24

so I have noticed more of them. But I am confident he could follow what I was saying in our conversation about leaving the house to Bruce, and I know he was able to reason about that and understood it and agreed it would be good to make this change."

"That's good enough for me, John. You see him regularly, and I see him only sporadically, when he calls me for some legal help, and he hasn't been calling me lately. I will get to work on this right away. Shouldn't take long to make that change, and I will let you know when the paperwork is ready to be signed. Good to talk with you and just let me know if you need anything else."

Ted sat for a moment, thinking. He had been a lawyer in his forties when he first took on Mr. Carr as a client, more than twenty years earlier. He was so bright, always ahead of the game, and he knew what he wanted, and he made all the calls on his own. It was hard to think of him as "slipping" mentally. He remembered, though, that not long ago his client had failed to pay a bill he had sent Mr. Carr for some legal work. He was a bit embarrassed to have to call and ask him to send a check, so he worked it through the butler who called it to Mr. Carr's attention. Maybe that was an example of one of those "little things" his brother John had in mind.

Ted called his younger partner, Rod Olson, and asked him to drop by and discuss updating the Carr Will. Rod worked almost exclusively on estate planning and wills,

and the last four or five of Zander's Wills and codicils had
been drafted by Rod. Ted used to do it himself, but estate
planning was not the focus of his practice, just something
he did to accommodate clients who wanted his personal
input. He was mainly an antitrust lawyer and a complex
litigation lawyer, with some memorable cases under his
belt. He also founded and headed up the patent and
intellectual property group in his Firm, one of the large
multi-state law firms that had developed a large South
Carolina presence. He was recognized in peer-review
surveys as a top-tier lawyer in multiple fields. People
teased him that he could not make up his mind what
area of the law he wanted to specialize in – a sore subject
with Ted, because he felt strongly that specialization had
been oversold. In his view, good judgment and careful
preparation were the critical factors in choosing a lawyer
for whatever type problem. Of course, specialization had
its place, but it was not for Ted. He had spent his career
successfully avoiding being pigeonholed in some narrow
field, and he was now a senior partner who could call
on younger specialists when needed, such as Rod Olson.
Still, he relished his role in making critical calls in all the
matters for which he was lead counsel. And he had pre-
vailed in some landmark cases while making those calls.

Rod came in, smiling, and said, "What's up, Ted?"
He had been working intermittently with Born on several
estate planning matters. "It's the Carr estate, Rod. Just
talked with Mr. Carr's brother John who relayed to me a
change Mr. Carr wants to make in his will - I gather with

a little input from John. Nothing wrong with that, of course. They are brothers, and he's Mr. Carr's Trustee of the living will and is set to be his Executor if he survives Mr. Carr. John seems in good health and his mind is sharp, but he is concerned his older brother is slipping. From what he says, Mr. Carr is still competent at this point, but we need to get this change made as soon as we can, because I gather he might be having some progressive problems, physically and maybe mentally. Seems to me it is best just to make a new will rather than a codicil amendment; it's simpler to probate, and it doesn't broadcast quite so loudly that Mr. Carr is removing the house from Bruce. This is not a punitive move relative to Bruce, just equity, but it might look like he was displeased with Bruce."

"Gotcha. I'll get right on it," Rod assured.

CHAPTER THREE

AT ZANDER'S HOUSE

Ted and Rod drove up to the imposing home of Alexander Carr. Ted had of course been to his home various times during the years of his representation of the man, but generally to leave documents or to have brief chats. Mostly, Mr. Carr had come to Ted's office to execute documents, for the convenience of having secretaries and notaries available, as well as typographical equipment to make any last-minute changes in paperwork. This time it was different, as Zander's new will, perhaps to be his last one, would be executed at home because Zander preferred not to have to make the trip downtown, with all the hassle. Ted and Rod were happy to bring the will out to him, and, if any changes were needed - which they did not expect - that would just have to be handled somehow.

Ted was driving, and he parked on the street in front of the house because he knew there would be other cars arriving, and the parking area behind the house was limited. As he and Rod walked up the long driveway from the street to the house, Ted took in the house in a way he never had before, partly because the house had been the subject of the most recent change in the will. It was a truly striking home. It sat on one of a pair of large estate-sized lots, the second lot vacant by design, adding to the magnificence of the expansive lawn. The house itself was two-storied, of brick and sculpted stone, and there were massive doors at each end of the red-tiled front porch, extending the entire front of the house, with a decorative black wrought iron railing along the porch and along the steps leading up to it. This was the formal approach to the house, rarely used by friends and relatives, who almost always entered though a side sunroom door.

How strange it seemed that this house had been the cause of Ted's original representation of Mr. Carr. He stopped at the top of the driveway and gazed at the house. "You know," Ted said to Rod, "Mr. Carr called me nearly 25 years ago because he had a tax problem with the house. He had bought the house from his parents, but they continued to live in the house, mainly because they were elderly and needed to be near their son for their care. They lived upstairs in a small area like a little apartment. Mr. Carr paid the taxes and utility bills and all the upkeep of the house, as he had already become wealthy by that time, and he gave his legendary parties there – when they were not held at his Club – all paid for by him personally. But the IRS determined that the purchase price was below the market value, and there had been no appraisal to establish fair value. The IRS took the position that the parents retained an interest in the house because they continued to live there after the purchase by Mr. Carr who, the IRS contended, had obtained it largely as a gift because he had allegedly bought it at sub-market value. As you can guess, the IRS included the entire value of the house (minus the amount Mr. Carr had paid) as a part of the parents' estate on their deaths, and the extra estate taxes would fall on Mr. Carr. That's when someone told him I had won a similar case earlier for another client, and he wanted to know if I could help him. Although you know I don't hold myself out as a tax lawyer, I took the case and we convinced the IRS that it was a real sale for fair value, with substance to it, and the house should not be included as a part of the parents' taxable estate. That is how I came to represent Mr. Carr, so many years ago, and now it is this house that is the subject of our trip here today."

"Those are not easy cases to win," Rod said. "So, I guess you became his lawyer from that time on. Right?" Ted nodded, and they proceeded to the formal entrance door, an exception to the usual routine, as the signing would take place in the living room on the front of the house. One of the staff let them into the foyer with the imposing staircase in front of them, the immense dining room to the left and the even larger living room with Austrian curtains at the windows and a gigantic Oriental rug with strong red overtones covering most of the hardwood floor. Mr. Carr had not come down just yet, but his brother John was there, and his accountant Joe Henaker was also there, to serve as a witness. Mr. Carr came down a few minutes later via an elevator that had been installed in an adjacent room, accompanied by the butler/chauffeur, Mr. Robbins.

Everyone sat down, and Ted said to his client, "Now, Mr. Carr, you know we are here today for you to execute a new will, if you agree this is what you want, and I will go over it with you in just a moment. Your brother John is here in case you want to talk with him first and ask him any questions, but then I am going to ask him to leave the room in a minute, because he is one of the beneficiaries under the will, and we never want anyone later saying that his presence intimidated you or unduly influenced anything about the will. Do you understand?"

"Yes, I understand," said Mr. Carr, "But I don't have any questions of John. Let's get on with the signing."

John left the room and went into the kitchen area to wait. Ted explained to Mr. Carr that this new will was just like the one that he last executed, except that his son Bruce would no longer inherit the house but that the house would go into his residuary estate and be sold, with the proceeds of the sale to be divided equally by all the children. Bruce, like each of the heirs, would have the right to buy the house from the estate by using a part of his inheritance to do so. Ted asked if this was the way he wanted it, and he said it was. Ted asked him a series of questions to assure that he understood the will and had the proper testamentary intent, and Ted and Rod were satisfied that he did. Then Ted asked him to sign his name at the end, and it was obvious that he was having painstaking problems writing the letters of his name and keeping the signature on the designated line. "That's my arthritis. It's terrible to be old," he said. Ted told him to take his time, that he was doing just fine. At last, the will was signed by Mr. Carr and was witnessed by Ted and Joe, and then Rod notarized it.

"Okay," said Ted, "we can now spring John out of purgatory and have him join us, and I understand he will be bringing something with him." John arrived, bearing a silver tray with small glasses and a choice of sherry or brandy. John was smiling pleasantly, slender build, male pattern balding in evidence, with a kind of string tie reminiscent of characters from western movies. "I think it is all settled now. Everything should be in good shape, and we can go on about our lives knowing that there has been good planning for the future. I propose a toast to everyone's good health, especially Zander's." "Hear, hear!" rang out the group as they raised their glasses.

Ted and Rod shortly gathered up the papers and left, assuring John and Zander that they would make copies for their legal files and would make additional file copies for Mr. Carr and John, retaining the original in their fireproof safe at the law office, as had been their custom.

Ted and Rod left and drove back to the office. "You know, Rod, I think this is the first time he has ever failed to extract assurance from me that I won't let Jesse have anything to do with his financial affairs. Maybe he is finally convinced he can count on me for that. Anyway, it looks like this might be the twelfth and last of Mr. Carr's wills and codicils that we have prepared. At least I feel good that everything is in place. We shouldn't have any problems after this," Ted said. "Let's hope not," Rod responded.

CHAPTER FOUR

AN EVENING WITH JOHN AND ANGELA

It was a Friday evening some two years later, about a week before Christmas, and the lovely home of John and Angela Carr was festively decorated for the Holidays, a large Frazier fir saturated with lights and ornaments dominating a corner of the living room, a holly and pine-cone arrangement on the mantle, and all manner of other seasonal decorations tastefully attesting to the coming of an expected very happy Christmas. It was just the two of them, looking forward to a quiet evening together. John had wanted to sit in the living room that night to enjoy the ambience, and he lighted the gas logs and put on some Christmas music, while Angela checked on the chicken tetrazzini in the kitchen.

John and Angela mainly favored white wine, one or two small glasses around dinnertime three or four times a week. But tonight, John thought an Old Fashioned with Bourbon, sugar, bitters and water would be the perfect Christmas-type drink, so he began fixing himself one, knowing that Angela would just prefer a glass of Chardonnay. He got inspired to add a bit of orange juice to his drink, and when he opened the refrigerator, he realized that they were about out of orange juice, perhaps only just enough left to do justice to his Old Fashioned. "Angela," he said, "Right after dinner, I will make a run to the Kwik Mart and get us some orange juice so we will have some for breakfast in the morning. I'm using the rest of what we have in the Fridge for my drink. But I can make a quick trip to the store."

"Okay," said Angela, "I meant to get some juice earlier today, but it slipped my mind. When you go to the Mart, could you also get us a quart of milk to use on our cereal in the morning? Looks like I have let us get low on breakfast fixings."

It was the beginning of what appeared to be an idyllic evening at home, enjoying the beauty of the living room, the soft background carols, the warm fire in the fireplace, and an Old Fashioned in one hand and a good book in the other. Angela joined him, in between trips to the kitchen, happy to have a quiet evening at home as a kind of oasis of the senses, after the hustle of a highly scheduled calendar of Christmas events and gatherings. The only discordant development was that John had begun to feel some indigestion, and he wondered what might have caused that problem.

During the break for dinner, John thought the indigestion might go away once he got some food in his stomach, but it persisted. John said nothing to Angela about this, didn't want to worry her, and certainly did not want her to think her beautiful dinner had caused it. After dinner, he told Angela he would go ahead to the nearby Kwik Mart before taking to his favorite chair again in the living room, just to get it behind him. He gathered his overcoat and hat, got in his sleek sedan and headed out the driveway in the cold night air.

After about forty-five minutes, Angela began to be concerned that it was taking John longer to pick up the couple of breakfast items and return home from the nearby Kwik Mart than she would have expected. Then she saw flashing blue lights of a car coming up her driveway. Two policemen stepped out of the car and came to the door. Angela's heart sank. "Ma'am, are you Angela Carr, and is your husband John Carr?" one of the officers asked. When a pale Angela nodded and faintly said "yes," the officer said, "I am sorry to have to tell you that your husband has had a serious accident, car ran off the road and struck a tree. He was unconscious when we found him, and non-responsive. Strangely, there isn't any sign he was speeding, and the car is damaged but not totaled. He has been taken to St. Bartholomew's Hospital.

I think you need to go check on him as soon as possible. We'll give you an escort if you feel able to drive your car." Angela, faint with shock, said she thought she could drive and that she knew she needed to have her car with her.

When they arrived at the hospital emergency room, Angela identified herself, and the attendant at the desk motioned Angela and the policemen through the door behind the desk. There they were met by two doctors and a nurse who told her, "I am so sorry. We have done everything we could do to resuscitate him, but we were unsuccessful. We can take you to the area where he is lying."

Angela began crying uncontrollably. "This couldn't have happened! It just couldn't have happened! We were having such a nice evening at home, and he just went to pick up a couple of items at the Kwik Mart. It just is impossible! It has to be a bad dream, a horrible nightmare!"

"We can't say for sure what happened, Mrs. Carr, but it does not appear that the impact of the crash injured him enough to cause this. He wasn't wearing his seat belt, but, even so, he did not seem to have sustained life-threatening injuries from the accident, though we can't be sure whether there were internal injuries we just have not identified yet. My guess is that he suffered a massive heart attack. Had he been having heart problems?" one of the physicians asked.

"Well, he had high blood pressure but was taking medicine for that, and something to help with cholesterol. He had by-pass surgery a couple of years ago, but we thought his heart problems were under control. I don't think he has had any symptoms lately," Angela tried to reflect through her sobs.

"Ma'am," said the lead policeman, "are there some family members we need to notify?" It was about 10:30 p.m., as the police began calling and summoning Zander's children to come to the hospital. Angela kept leaning over and kissing John on the forehead as he lay on the table. "We have to make funeral arrangements, and what a terrible thing to have to do, with Christmas right upon us. We'll do well to be able to make funeral arrangements at the Church with just a few days before Christmas. At least we know the burial location; he will be buried in one of the Carr family plots at the cemetery." Zander's children who lived in and near Greenville were there with Angela as they said their goodbyes and released his body to the undertaker. Angela spent the night with one of the children.

CHAPTER FIVE

TED BORN GETS A MESSAGE

Ted and Lydia had left on the same Friday before Christmas to visit their daughter Rebecca Born Stockton and her family in Charleston. It was a good visit, with Ted playing chess with grandson Tom and working on a Christmas tree jigsaw puzzle with granddaughters Fran and Kat, as well as listening to the grandchildren play Christmas music on piano and guitar. All seemed so right and wonderful. Then, the next morning, Ted got an email message from his law partner Rod Olson that read: "Ted, I know you are out of town, but I opened the newspaper this morning and there was an obituary of JOHN CARR! It seems he had a car accident last Friday evening, but the obituary just got into the newspaper this morning, on Christmas Eve. The family has already had a memorial service and burial – must have had to rush it because of Christmas – but I knew nothing about it at the time. Of course, we did not handle John's personal legal work, just his brother's, so I guess no one thought to notify us. I'm sure you know what this means: You, Ted, are now Mr. Carr's Trustee, attorney-in-fact, and his potential Executor. We need to talk as soon as possible when you get back after Christmas."

Ted stopped and looked blankly into the distance, stunned by the news. He would now have responsibilities he had not expected to have, and he was not sure quite how to step into his new role. He was sorry about John's death and wanted more information about it. It struck him that he really did not know any of Zander's children, even though they were in line to inherit Mr. Carr's assets, as Born had dealt only with Mr. Carr and John on the estate planning. The children had been abstractions up to now, but he would surely be interacting with them in the future. He barely knew John's widow Angela. He thought it would probably look like he was prying if he called Angela now, and it might even be taken as an effort to solicit the legal handling of John's estate work. Anyway, tomorrow was Christmas Day, and he was out of town and could do nothing until he returned to Greenville. A thousand questions raced through Ted's mind. He had successfully handled many high stakes litigations, and he had collected many kudos as a first rate go-to lawyer when the client just HAD to win, and this matter in many ways would be small in comparison, he thought. But it was very different; it was a highly personal matter in a way that was not at all like dealing with his large corporate clients. In a sense, he had now become his own client – a big change.

On his return to Greenville, his first order of business was to visit Mr. Carr. He was ushered by the butler/chauffeur into his upstairs sitting room, a very unpretentious room upstairs in the great house, sparsely furnished in contrast with the elaborate furnishing of the downstairs living area. Ted supposed that the room must not have changed much since the time it had served as the bedroom for Mr. Carr's mother, during her lifetime. He approached Mr. Carr, feeling differently from his usual prior attorney-client meetings, and said, "Mr. Carr, I am so very sorry about the passing of your brother John. I know you and he were close and that you counted on him to be around when you needed things done. I was out of town when it happened and knew nothing about it until the memorial service was all over. I offer my deepest sympathy and condolences to you. I will miss him, too, as we worked very well together."

Mr. Carr looked blankly out a window and just said, "I wish I knew more about what happened."

"I don't know much about that, either – just got back in town," said Ted. "But, as you know, I was your alternate to John, and I want to assure you that I will do everything possible to carry on and do for you whatever you need. I will do my best to take good care of you."

"Thank you, Ted. I need all the help I can get," he replied.

"Well, I need to go now, but you and your staff have all my contact information to reach me when you need me, and of course I will be back to see you when we get things in order." Mr. Carr nodded, and Ted began to leave the room, as one of relatives came in, introduced to Ted as Mr. Carr's grandson Kimbo, son of Mr. Carr's eldest son Kim, exchanging brief greetings.

Back at the office, Ted sat down with Rod Olson to review the landscape with Ted's new roles as Trustee, holder of the power of attorney, and future Executor. "Here's the situation as I see it," Ted began. "I never thought this was going to happen, and I am not sure I like it. But here I am, and I think I'm obligated to see it through. But I've got a few problems. First, I'm not a family member, and I don't have immediate casual access to Mr. Carr like his brother John had, and I also do not have a good handle on Mr. Carr's mental and emotional condition. I know he was beginning to have dementia a couple of years ago, according to John – you know, when we last revised his will to deal with the disposition of the homeplace. Presumably, the dementia has been advancing, but I am not sure how far. Now, John could just walk in at any time and say, 'Zander, we need to do this or that,' or 'I'll handle such-and-such and you can forget about it,' and I am sure he had no problem just taking charge. But suppose I walked into his sitting room and began taking over his affairs and hiring and firing his staff – if it came to that. If he is really far gone, he might just nod and accept it. But if he has enough mental capacity to feel that he can still manage things, at least up to a point, he could be very offended by a 'take charge' attitude on my part. So, I am going to have to be very diplomatic in my new role and feel my way along. In a way, my job is going to be more complicated than it was for John. Plus, I am still practicing law full time. I have a bunch of other clients who are expecting me to be taking care of their matters. So, I can't be on the scene all that often. I need to figure out a way to see that bills get paid and that he is taken care of, even when I am not on the scene. I'm new at this and you handle this kind of stuff all the time. I need your suggestions."

"Well, suggestion number one would be to remember that, in your position as Trustee, power of attorney holder, and potentially as his Executor-in-waiting, you have fiduciary duties to Mr. Carr to take reasonable measures for the preservation and protection of his assets," Rod offered. "For one thing, he has these employees that everyone calls the 'staff.' As I understand it, he has a butler/chauffeur who has been with him for years and is probably trustworthy. Then he has a cook who has been with him a year or two, and he has two or three around-the-clock sitters, at least one or two of them fairly recent hires, I think. Besides that, he has people who mow his lawn and do some shrubbery trimming and pruning, and various maintenance people who come into the house from time to time. And then there are the family members who will drop in whenever the spirit moves them. My point is that Mr. Carr has a lot of valuable items in his house, including jewelry, and jewelry is easy to misappropriate. A lot of valuable things, like rings and pins and bracelets - even necklaces that belonged to his wife – can easily be slipped into someone's pocket and taken away and hocked or sold. And they might never be missed, or, if they are missed, it might be only when Mr. Carr passes away - by that time, all tracks of the theft have possibly been lost. I don't think he goes out much anymore, and rarely wears much jewelry, other than his fine watch and a couple of rings. He won't know anything is missing, and no one else will know either, except the ones who have taken the items. You need to find a way to protect his personal property; otherwise, you might be liable for negligence in the performance of your duties. Now, being diplomatic is fine, and I think you should be diplomatic, but the bottom line is to protect his assets."

"I know you are right about that, but it's easier said than done. One problem I have is that I don't really know the children, nor Jesse. Aside from avoiding offense to Mr. Carr, I have to be sensitive as to whether his children and other close relatives will resent, and perhaps be suspicious of, anything and everything I do. They could prove to be a problem," Ted said thoughtfully. "I think I will start by talking with his CPA, Joe Henaker, and make sure I understand how they have been working things out up to now, just mechanical things, like keeping track of the hours the employees work and getting them their checks, and making sure the withholding taxes get paid, and the matching contributions, and vacation pay and sick leave. And all that. You know, there is a lot of paperwork that must be done for the Government. Then we will take it one day at a time."

"Obviously, you hold Mr. Carr's power of attorney. Do you anticipate using that, other than in securing his personal property, and maybe managing his financial accounts outside the Trust?" asked Rod.

Ted hesitated for a moment and then said, "Ordinarily, I regard a power of attorney as a last resort kind of thing. I don't want to use it unless Mr. Carr tells me to use it or unless I conclude that he cannot function, in which case I would have no choice but to use it. I don't have a good enough feel at this point whether he has crossed the line where I need to use it to take over the full responsibility of his care. A power of attorney is a powerful thing that can be abused, and I certainly don't want Mr. Carr to think I am using it in situations where he could still make the decisions for himself. It is just one of those 'one-day-at-a-time' kinds of things. I'll have to feel my way through a lot of this."

"How are you going to bill for your work, and the firm's work in support of you?" asked Rod.

"Just the way I always have. We will just bill for our time at our usual hourly rates. No one should have a problem with that," said Ted. "Well, just give this whole situation some thought, and I will be thinking about it, and we will come up with a plan." Rod left the room, and Ted immediately put in a call to the CPA. "Hi, Joe, this is Ted Born. Sorry I was out of town when John Carr died, a fine man, and so sad, especially for Angela. But that means I'm Mr. Carr's Trustee, and potentially his Executor, if I survive him, and I hold his power of attorney in case I need to exercise it actively. I do think I have to identify and secure his personal property, given doubts about his mental state. I don't relish the job, but he wanted me to be his alternate, and I agreed to it. He really didn't have anyone else."

"No, he really didn't. It just wouldn't work for any of the family members to serve - God forbid that Jesse would step in, but there were problems with his children handling it, as well. He's always thought the world of you," Joe volunteered.

"In any event, I committed to do it, and so here I am. Joe, how are the payrolls being handled right now for the staff, and how are the bills getting paid?" Ted inquired.

"We have it set up so that the butler, Earl Robbins, keeps track of the staff hours, and he turns in the numbers every week to a payroll service. I look over the numbers to see if they seem right or in-line, and I ask questions of Robbins if anything seems out of line. When I approve it, the checks are written and given to the staff, and Mr. Carr's bank reimburses the payroll service and pays for their services. That's how we handle it," Henaker explained.

"Okay. I assumed you had some sort of system like that. But how about buying groceries and other items needed around the house, how's that handled?" Henaker said there was a credit tab at the hardware store where the butler could go and get what was needed, and an itemized bill would be sent to Henaker which he would check to see if the items and the cost seemed reasonable. As for groceries, Mr. Robbins was given a petty cash sum to buy groceries and other items. Henaker would review the tabs for purchases and would authorize the replenishing of the petty cash to bring it back up to the authorized level. "Sounds like a pretty good system, Joe. And you had this same system going, I assume, all the time John served as his Trustee and attorney-in-fact?" Henaker affirmed that it had indeed been in place all through John Carr's tenure, with a few refinements from time to time. Ted thought this was not only a good and responsible system, but he also was glad John Carr had set it up, because it would be hard for anyone to object to Ted's continuation of a system that John Carr had instituted. "Let's just continue the way you are doing it, and don't hesitate to contact me if you run into any problems. I look forward to working with you, Joe."

The next day, Ted got a telephone from Randolph Carr, the youngest of Alexander Carr's three sons. After identifying himself, Rand, as he was called, said, "After my Uncle John's death, I went to the stock brokerage office to check on the status of Dad's accounts that Uncle John had been handling, and they told me that you were now Dad's Trustee. I just thought it would be good to meet you and talk about how things would be handled in the future."

"That's absolutely fine, Rand. I look forward to meeting you, and I can even see you this afternoon, if you like," Ted responded. They agreed that Rand would come to Ted's office to see him at about 3:00 p.m. Rand appeared at Ted's office promptly at the appointed time, accompanied by his wife, Tammy. Ted thought that Rand was a bit testy, although he was polite. Rand wanted to know how it came about that Ted was his dad's Trustee, and Ted explained that Mr. Carr had asked Ted years ago to be his alternate Executor and then, when the living trust was set up, he also asked Ted to be his alternate Trustee. Ted avoided disclosing reasons given by Mr. Carr, in confidence, as to why he had not chosen a family member. Rand asked if Ted felt comfortable doing the job of Trustee since he was not a family member. Ted replied that he had no doubt he could do it, as he had promised Mr. Carr, and he hoped to be in close contact with family members so that they would have confidence he was doing his job properly, and that he welcomed their input. Then Rand asked the question that it appeared he had come to ask: "How much are you going to charge for your work as Trustee?" Ted replied, "I am going to continue to charge for my time just as I always have done in my work for your dad." When Ted said those words, there was a visible gulp from Tammy, and moments of silence from both Rand and Tammy, as they looked at each other. They then said they needed to go, excusing themselves.

CHAPTER SIX

"WE NEED A FAMILY MEMBER"

"Dammit, Tammy," Rand Carr said to his wife. "I don't like this. I don't know anything about this guy Ted Born except he has a reputation as a high-powered lawyer. He's an outsider who is messing around in the concerns of our family. What he's *not* is, he's not a member of the family, and as things stand, we've all got to work through him. Just take, for instance, this bank loan we have on our house. Sometimes we have payments coming due, like our second mortgage payment right now, and it was always good to know we could possibly get help from Dad, if we need it. I can't get any help from Uncle John's estate, because Aunt Angela needs to have those assets preserved, and my sister Kate, as Uncle John's Executrix, would never agree to advance me the money. She thinks we should just sell this house, saying we can't afford it and it should be sold and then we should buy a cheaper house. If I need to go to Dad for help, it looks like I have to go through this lawyer, and I don't know what his attitude might be. It would be tough enough if Uncle John was here, managing Dad's assets, because I'm not sure he would approve it. But he would have been a better bet than this lawyer. I don't know, I just don't know whether the lawyer would help or not, and if he refused, we would be up a creek without a paddle!"

"Obviously, we need to try to find a way to get him out – and, by the way, he's going to cost us money, big time. Did you hear him say he was going to charge regular legal fees? I wonder how much that could be," Tammy offered.

"Yeah, that's another thing," Rand agreed. "I need to talk with Uncle John's lawyer that's handling his estate, Jason Smith. Need to see what he thinks of the situation, and he can give us a good idea what Ted Born will be costing us. How about if I give him a call right now?" Rand picked up the phone and dialed Smith's office and got him on the line immediately. "Jason, this is Rand Carr. I know it's late in the afternoon, but I hope you have a few minutes. Tammy and I have just gotten back from a visit to meet and talk with Ted Born, who we found out is the Trustee of Dad's living trust and holds his power of attorney. By the way, do you know him?"

"Not well, Rand, not so well personally, but of course I know him by reputation. He is certainly reputed to be a fine lawyer. In fact, your Dad and your Uncle John spoke so highly of him, I was a bit concerned that your Uncle John would switch his own estate's legal work to Born. But that never happened. How did your meeting go?" Smith asked.

"Actually, we did not go into much detail in the meeting. Tammy and I just wanted to see who he was, put a face with his name, and get a feel for what we could expect. It's strange to be dealing with someone who is not a family member, someone you do not even know, who now has control of your Dad's assets, both now and after he passes. I did ask him about what his charges would be for his work, and he said he would make standard charges, or something to that effect. So, he's not going to do his work gratis. We were wondering whether you could give us an idea what he might cost us, what he would be dipping out of Dad's estate. What do you think he might charge?" Rand asked.

"Rand, I don't know what he might charge. The law does put an upper limit on what he could charge, you know, a maximum percentage of estate assets. And he will have two jobs, first managing the assets and the trust during the remainder of your Dad's life, and then managing his estate after he is gone. Considering your Dad's wealth, you could be looking at a fee request of up to a million dollars. If he asks for that much, there is a fair chance the Probate Court might approve it and award him that much. You know, the Court would have to review and approve or disapprove the fee, and you would have the right to object. But, considering Zander's wealth, the Court might well approve a million bucks, especially if there are complications, and I can see there would be the potential for complications. Of course, Ted might not request a fee of that size," Smith advised.

"A cool million dollars? WOW! That's quite a fee! And for someone we really don't know or need. A family member could handle this at no cost at all. It is so unnecessary! Well, thanks for the input, Jason. We'll just have to think about this. I appreciate your taking my call late in the day, but this has been very helpful. Just put your charges for this call on your overall charges for Uncle John's estate, and thanks!" Rand stroked his forehead and brow and said to his wife, "Tammy, this Ted Born could cost us a million dollars. We've got a lot of thinking and talking to do."

The next day, Rand was on the phone with his brothers, making the case that the Carr family had no need for an outsider to manage their Dad's affairs, that a family member could do that, and Born was going to charge a million dollars for possibly being mainly an obstacle to the family members' access to their Dad's wealth. Rand got the feeling that they mostly might be amenable to an effort to get Born out of the picture. Then he called his sister Kate Carr Ross. Kate's reaction was more cautious,

"Rand, you might be right, but the estate is going to have to have a lawyer, even if a family member is Trustee and Executor, and if the lawyer can also serve in those capacities, there might not be much difference in costs. Also, I can't get it out of my mind that our Dad knew full well what was in the Trust and the Will - he knew Ted Born was the alternate and chose him for that purpose – and he did not make or suggest any change, and always spoke highly of Born. And what's the alternative, who would be the family member to do the work if he got replaced? There is going to be a lot of work, and I know I can't do it. I'm handling Uncle John's estate, plus being a wife and mother and doing a lot of other things, and I don't know which of us would step in and take on the responsibilities – and the *work*," Kate observed thoughtfully.

"We'll figure that out. Do you know this lawyer Ted Born?" Rand asked.

"I don't know him, but I know his wife," Kate responded. "She's a member of one of the organizations I belong to. Seems to be very nice. And, of course, I know Dad knew and had a high regard for Mr. Born. That's a good enough recommendation for me." Kate agreed that she would at least attend a family meeting to discuss the whole situation.

CHAPTER SEVEN

BELLING THE CAT

Ted was meeting with Rod Olson again. "Rod, I had a short meeting yesterday with Rand Carr and his wife Tammy. It was just an introductory meeting, as they said they just wanted to meet me. But I had an uneasy feeling the meeting did not go well. When they asked me what I would be charging for my services, I told them I would just continue billing my regular fees, just as I always had done for Mr. Carr's work. I thought this would reassure them that I was not planning to charge some percentage of the assets fee, but they seemed surprised, and I noticed that Tammy noticeably swallowed very hard at my answer. They promptly got up and left, never said 'thank you' or 'we look forward to working with you and seeing more of you.' Of course, I could have misread their reaction, but it convinced me that one of our priorities should be to have a meeting with all the children, and I would even include Jesse in the meeting also, since he, after all, is Mr. Carr's brother. I will try to set that up shortly."

Rod agreed, "Yeah, I think that would be a good idea, clear the air, make sure they know we are going to be fair and conscientious, answer any questions, and get off to a good start. That dovetails into the other thing you and I mentioned relative to the securing of Mr. Carr's assets. We ought to invite them all to our inventorying of the assets. This would be a demonstration of transparency that would build trust. Where do we stand on that project?"

"Here's where we are at the moment," Ted answered. "What we need is to take all of Mr. Carr's valuables, one-by-one, assign a number to each one and photograph it with the assigned number on a card placed next to the item being photographed, so that the item and each assigned number will show up in the photograph. Then we need to dictate a record providing a verbal description of the item and an estimate of value, all keyed to the assigned number of the item. We will include antique furniture, paintings, and larger valuables as well as jewelry. After we have done that, we will take all the relatively small items, put them in individual transparent plastic baggies, with their assigned number accompanying each one in the baggies. I have rented a very large safe deposit box at the bank, and we will put all the small items, mainly jewelry and some silverware, in the safe deposit box where my signature and one other person's signature is required in order to open it – except, of course, we will leave at the house any items Mr. Carr uses often, such as the engraved sterling silver pen and pencil set, his watch, a couple of rings – a few things like that. If the safe deposit box gets opened, for example, to allow a family member to get access to an item of jewelry for some special occasion, we will put a note in the safe deposit box signed by the borrower, identifying the piece taken. Of course, we can't do that with pieces of antique furniture or paintings, but there is not much risk that someone will walk out of the house with the massive French buffet, or even one of the Sèvres vases. Everyone will be invited to observe the entire inventorying and protective process, and I think the family would be reassured that we are taking good care of Mr. Carr's valuables, which one day will go mostly to them as legacies."

"Sounds good," said Rod. "But who's going to describe the items and put an estimated value on them? And have we got any idea how Mr. Carr will react to any of this?"

"I've gotten in touch with the jeweler favored by the family, the one that has actually sold him and his diseased wife a lot of fine items over the years, and he will dictate the description and a value estimate as each item is photographed, referencing the number assigned to the item. We will do this on a Sunday when he does not have to be in the store, and that will work well also with the secretary who will be transcribing his dictation. I know one of our new lawyers at the Firm, Tim Laird, has super-duper camera equipment and he can do the photographing. We will have a white cloth on Mr. Carr's dining room table, where the items will be placed for photographing. As far as Mr. Carr is concerned, I am not sure how he will take it. It helps that we will be doing this on Sunday, when he has no medical appointments or other events that might interfere with the work, and he generally spends almost all day every day in his upstairs sitting room. The cook takes lunch up to him. I am not sure whether I ought to mention this to Mr. Carr in advance, because I am not sure he would understand. I tend to think it might go best if we just get the butler, Mr. Robbins, to tell him that some pictures are being taken of some valuables for security purposes and leave it at that. Robbins knows where all the valuables are, and he can bring them to us as we need them, without making a big fuss over it. If Mr. Carr gets upset, I will just have to go upstairs and speak to him and try to get him to understand that we are taking pictures because we think it is a good idea to have a record in case anything gets lost or goes missing, for insurance purposes, if for nothing else - which is very truthful, as this is much needed for insurance protection."

"So, do you want me to be there?" Rod asked. "Yes, indeed," replied Ted. "I need you as a witness. And I am going to ask Joe Henaker, the CPA, to come also, and in fact it is his secretary who will be transcribing the dictation, as she is very good at handling technical terms that might be used in the descriptions. If she isn't sure she has the spelling right to some technical descriptions, she will make sure she gets them right and verified before she leaves the house. I think I will also invite the estranged brother Jesse Carr to come, just out of courtesy. He is a small beneficiary under the will, though just a modest amount of cash, no valuable personal property."

Ted picked up the phone and called Rand Carr, explained his concerns about securing the valuables and asked him to invite his siblings to come, as well as his Uncle Jesse. Rand promised to do so, and said he thought it would be well to ask Jason Smith to come as well, since he was advising the siblings in connection with the probate of John Carr's estate. Ted said he thought that would be a great idea, and he added that he wanted to schedule a meeting with all of Rand's brothers and sister just to get their input about going forward and to share Ted's own thoughts about how to proceed. Rand said that would be a good idea but was not sure when they could do it.

Immediately after the telephone conversation with Ted Born, Rand got on the phone with each of his brothers and sister and Uncle Jesse and told them of the inventorying of valuables. All but one of them said they could come. But then he told them that it looked like Born was rapidly moving in to take charge of their Dad's affairs, and that they all urgently needed to get together to decide how to deal with Born. Rand said he thought it was urgent, and could they meet tomorrow. Surprisingly, most of them said they could make such a meeting, even on such short notice, the meeting to be at the house of Rand and Tammy.

The Carr "children" ranged in age from about 45 to 60, and most of them had adult children or teenagers. Some of them brought their spouses to the meeting Rand had called. Uncle Jesse, at age 86, was there as well. Rand began the meeting by saying that, as everyone knew, lawyer Ted Born had Zander's power of attorney and might have suggested having himself named as the alternate to Uncle John, so he could get a huge fee, maybe around a million dollars. Rand said in his opinion Born had no business being involved in the Carr family affairs, that he would be expensive, and that some member of the Carr family could handle things just as well, if not better, and without charge. He went on to say that Born was moving fast to "take over" things, and soon he would be locked in and probably could not be removed. If the family wanted to make a change, this was the time to do it; they needed to move quickly.

"If you are right, Rand, what do you propose we do?" asked Kim, the oldest of the children.

"There's only one thing that we can do: Get Dad to revoke the power of attorney and name one of us. Then, once we get the power of attorney and oust Born from his day-to-day control, we can get the Trust and the Will changed," answered Rand. That process would get Born out of the picture.

"Well, that might not be so easy to do. In the first place, Dad has always had a mind of his own. He likely won't appreciate one of us trying to get him to change his estate plans. Second, who will we ask Dad to name as his power of attorney? I'm not a candidate, just have no interest in doing it. And from my observations, Dad still thinks of us as the children he knew as we were growing up, and I am not at all sure he would think of us as good power of attorney candidates," observed Kim.

Rand had a ready answer: "Okay, you've all accused me of being Dad's favorite, which I doubt — he's always been very receptive to Kate. But I do visit him a lot and run errands and do favors for him, and I have been around him enough, especially after Uncle John's death, to tell you that he is no longer the tough and independent-minded Dad we grew up with. He has been losing it mentally and mellowing over the last few years, and Uncle John's death was devastating to him and has accelerated his problems. He feels alone. He feels vulnerable. He feels helpless and is reaching out for whatever help he can get. I feel pretty sure that, if we take a new power of attorney to him and tell him we need him to sign this so we will be able to help him better, he will sign it. Then we give a copy of the new power of attorney to Ted Born and tell him to stay away from Dad, as we exercise our power of attorney to protect him and his interests. And we will tell the staff, and especially Earl Robbins, not to let Born in the house, that he is not welcome there."

Kim continued with his questioning. "Who's going to draw up this power of attorney? I doubt if Jason Smith would do it because he thinks too much of Born. He might feel that Born would think Smith was doing this so he could squeeze out Born and take over the representation of Dad, and I know he would not want to get into a lawsuit with Born."

"I know a lawyer," Rand said, "that I play golf with who does this kind of estate planning work. I think I could get him to do it, and I think he would understand that he would be promoting justice by displacing a money-grubbing lawyer who took advantage of a client and who has written himself a ticket to Dad's assets."

"You might be right about some of this, Rand, but you are wrong about one thing. Born wasn't given Dad's power of attorney or named as his alternate Trustee and Executor because Born took advantage of him. Dad never, ever, let anyone take advantage of him. You can bet he knew what he was doing and did exactly what he intended to do. Dad always had a reason for everything he did. Furthermore, Uncle John would not have stood for it if he had not been convinced it was what Dad wanted, and that it was a legitimate choice. So, if we do take some action like this, let's not fool ourselves into thinking we are rescuing Dad from some sort of entrapment Born pulled on him. We would be doing it only because we think it's in our interest, to hell with what Dad thought or wanted." Kim continued.

"Okay, Kim, maybe Dad did put Born's name on the documents intentionally. But that was a long time ago, and times and circumstances have changed, and he has a right to change his mind because it is obvious that Dad needs a family member as his power of attorney holder. We would still be acting in his interest, and I think he would agree if he still had all his faculties."

Kate interjected herself into the discussion. "Look, Rand, on the one hand you say Dad is not at himself, that he is vulnerable and will sign whatever we put in front of him, and then you say he has the right to change his mind. But I am not sure he has the capacity to make a considered decision to change his mind. We would just be substituting OUR minds for his. That's not quite right, and remember, Dad thought Born should be the alternate to Uncle John. I am sure Uncle John would have worked to convince Dad to make a change if he had not agreed Born was the right choice."

"Kate, be realistic. It's just not right - it's plain not workable for us to have to deal with this stranger, who's going to get rich off our family assets. The practicalities dictate that we need to make a change, and I think we can do it," Rand responded.

Bruce Carr spoke up: "Rand, do you remember the old fable about the mice sitting around in a group, like we are doing, and they came up with a wonderful plan to put a bell around the neck of the cat so they would get a warning from the tinkling bell and scurry to safety when the cat came near them. They just had one problem: Who was going to bell the cat? Aren't we at that point right now where this plan of changing the power of attorney is not going anywhere unless we can decide who's going to bell the cat – who's going to go to Dad and get him to sign this new power of attorney?"

Rand smiled. "I've thought about that, Bruce, and I have a candidate. I haven't discussed this with him yet, but I propose Uncle Jesse, who is right here with us. Now, I can anticipate what some of you are thinking: Uncle Jesse and Dad have not been on good terms, and, Uncle Jesse, at first thought you would not seem to be a good prospect for belling the cat but hear me out. Two things have changed. First, Uncle John has passed away, and Dad misses the hell out of him, and he's lonely and miserable and is looking for help, sympathy, understanding and attention from anyone who will give it. Second, he will relate to his brother of 86 years and in his present state of mind, he won't be thinking about the estrangement, or he will minimize it and look beyond it. Uncle Jesse, you are my nominee. You are the one. Will you take this on?"

Jesse had been sitting quietly, assuming that, as usual, he was automatically sidelined from involvement in anything relating to Zander. If he was ever invited to one of Zander's parties, it was out of the social obligation or politeness, and he knew that he was expected to blend into the shadows. He had been a failure in business and had survived, but with a struggle, and he knew Zander got respect that no one accorded to younger brother Jesse. Now, finally, someone had suggested a way that he could, more or less, take charge, and he would be respected and looked up to. Yet he was surprised and unsure this would work out. He said, "Interesting thought, Rand. I sort of thought I really ought to play some role in this situation, because I don't think we need Born, and I don't think he is the right person for Zander or for the rest of the family. Is he going to come by every day and visit with Zander? Is he going to check on Zander's arthritis or see that he has plenty of his favorite strawberry ice cream? Jesse Carr would do that. In fact, I want to do it. It would fill a void in my life, to feel like I was taking care of my brother. I always admired him, but I always felt he looked down on me because I had not been a business success, and there was some resentment there. But I am 86 years old, and we don't have time for any more past resentment, but just enough time to deal with the present and future. I would like to take care of Zander in our declining years. I'm willing to give it a try."

"Okay," said Rand, "are we then all in agreement that Uncle Jesse should try to make this happen?"

The reaction was mixed, but no one was willing to say "no," and no one had any better suggestions. Jesse just had one condition. He wanted everyone's support when he approached Zander with the new power of attorney. Rand added, "It might take a few days to get the power of attorney thing worked out, and in the meantime, Born has scheduled this inventory deal. I would say let that go forward as scheduled, because it needs to be done anyway, and Born apparently has all the arrangements made out. So, we will do that on Sunday. Everybody is invited, but if you can't make it, it's not a big deal. I'm going to be there, and I assume you can be there, Uncle Jesse, and anyone else who can be there probably should come, even if you can't stay for the whole thing. You will get to see and meet Born. You know, he wants to have a meeting with us to introduce himself and answer our questions, and I can put him off, reminding him he essentially will be meeting us at the inventorying. He has no idea that it will not be necessary for him ever to meet with us in some conference room, if our plan works out. I feel confident of that," Rand smiled knowingly.

Sunday came, and the inventorying went fairly smoothly. Box lunches had been brought so that there would be no need to interrupt the work to go out for lunch. Jesse was there, pacing the floor nervously, not interested in or taking part as an observer or otherwise in the work that was going on. At one point, Jesse pulled Born aside and said, "Can you send me a copy of the Trust and the Will? I would just like to see it, and I think as a member of the family I should be able to see it." Ted Born did not welcome this request, especially as Jesse was a marginal beneficiary, but in the interest of transparency he said he would do so, subject to checking on the ethics of revealing a client's estate planning documents to others without the consent of the client. He would check out the ethical problem and would be back in touch, he told Jesse. Mr. Carr remained in his sitting room during the inventorying and did not interfere with the work, only once calling down to see when his lunch would be brought up. Jason Smith was there as the lawyer for John's estate and as a friend of Zander's children, and he approved of Born's handling of the documentation. After the valuables had been photographed and gathered for placement in the safe deposit box Born had opened, Smith said he was perfectly trusting of Born to place the valuables in the box on the following day, as the banks were not open on Sunday. Born carried this responsibility out and breathed a sigh of relief that the valuables were now secure, and he would have an excellent record of all of them, with photographs and accompanying information, to identify and be able to retrieve specific items if necessary. All would be documented in a thick black notebook containing the photographs of items, alongside the descriptive information.

Later that Monday, Born received a call from Rand Carr that Rand would like to come by and see him, and Born accommodated his request and received Rand into his law office later that afternoon. Rand explained he needed a short-term loan from his Dad relative to a mortgage payment that was coming due. His sister Kate had told him that John Carr's estate could not be looked to for such funds. So, it was his Dad or else he was in big trouble. Born told Rand he would have to study the trust document to see if he would be authorized to approve such a loan.

Ted told Rand that, in any event, if he made the loan, he would make it only if Mr. Carr would sign off on it, as he did not believe it was a proper loan when not secured with specific and adequate collateral. Born studied the trust document and his power of attorney and concluded that such a loan would be problematic, but of course it could be made if Mr. Carr would approve it. Born went to see Mr. Carr about this request on behalf of Rand. Born was sympathetic with Rand's situation, but he doubted his own legal authority to authorize the loan without the express approval of Mr. Carr. Although Mr. Carr had been generous to Rand and his siblings in the past, it was possible he would draw the line on this one. He almost did. Ted thought it would be wise to approach Mr. Carr outside the presence of Rand Carr to try to smooth the way, before bringing Rand in. When Ted explained that Rand had come to him with an urgent request for funds to meet a mortgage payment, Mr. Carr almost exploded, saying, "Well, he can just go somewhere else. I don't have that kind of money." Ted responded, "Mr. Carr, it is your money, and you can certainly make the decision not to lend it, but just in case you think you might not have that much available, I do want to be sure you know that you do have that amount and much more. I am not pushing you to lend him the money, but I did not want you to make the decision on the belief that you don't have the money, because you do. Rand says he is afraid he might lose his house." Mr. Carr was silent for a moment and then he said, "Well, I don't want him to lose his house. I guess I ought to do it." Ted reiterated that it was Mr. Carr's decision to make, and he inquired if he was sure he wanted to make the loan. Resignedly, he said he did. Ted assured him he would prepare a note and other loan documents, and that Mr. Carr would need to sign a letter of authorization to his stockbroker directing that a check for the loan be made payable to Rand Carr. Ted told him that he and Rand would be coming back to see him to get everything signed.

The next day, Rand Carr met Ted Born at Mr. Carr's home and went up to his sitting room. There was a large rectangular magnifying glass, like a small windowpane set up at about eye level so that Mr. Carr could peer through it and try to read documents, although the butler had told Ted earlier that he had largely given up trying to read anything. It had been painful to give up his reading because he had always been an avid reader of the *New York Times*, as well as a couple of more local newspapers, subscriptions he still maintained even though the papers now were discarded, unread, in the trash. However, the contraption was somewhat helpful in connection with signing Zander's name. Even with the magnification, he could not see the line where he was supposed to put his signature. Ted had to take a felt pen and draw a heavy black line where he was to sign. Then Mr. Carr began the labored process of trying to sign his name. It took some anxious moments to watch him attempt the signing. He kept asking if his letters were "on the line," and in truth they wandered above and below the line, but Ted assured him it was all right. It was painful to watch, and Ted thought how much more difficult this effort was, compared with the last time he had seen Mr. Carr sign, when the will had been revised to remove the gift of the house. But the letter of authorization did get signed with a crude and strange-looking signature, and Rand signed the note and loan papers, which Ted put in his briefcase. They both thanked Mr. Carr, and Ted and Rand jointly went to the brokerage office and got a check for Rand.

Ted wondered if he had done the right thing, but he thought this action was consistent with Mr. Carr's past generosity toward Rand and his siblings, and he had enough cognition to feel he did not want Rand to lose his house. It would also possibly help Rand have a more positive feeling toward Ted in Ted's new role as Mr. Carr's attorney-in-fact, and Trustee. However, he thought he probably should make it clear to all the Carr children that it was unlikely he would approve any other loans to family members, at least not without good security of the type a commercial lending institution would require. One more early crisis behind him, he thought.

CHAPTER EIGHT

JESSE DROPS A BOMBSHELL

It was two days after Ted had arranged the loan for Rand Carr that Ted's secretary stepped into his office and said, "I have a Mr. Jesse Carr on the line, and he says it is very urgent he come in to see you this morning as soon as possible. You have another appointment at 10:30." Ted said, "I wonder what is so urgent. But tell him I can see him now if he can come right on; otherwise, it will have to be after lunch." Jesse said he would be right down.

Jesse did come and was ushered into Ted's office. "Hi, Mr. Carr," Ted said, "What can I do for you?" Jesse said nothing, but he tossed a document across Ted's desk. Ted picked it up, looked it over, and said, "This paper looks like a power of attorney by Mr. Alexander Carr designating you as his attorney-in-fact, and naming Rand Carr in some capacity – it's not clear whether the two of you are named as co-attorneys-in-fact or whether Rand is an alternate who would succeed you. Jesse just said, "Well, what do you think about it?"

"I really don't know, Mr. Carr," Born responded. "I will have to give it some thought. I am his Trustee, too, you know. How did this all come about?"

Jesse, with studied hostility, replied, "He just wants me to be his power of attorney, not you. That's all you need to know. And I asked you to send me a copy of that Trust and the Will, and you haven't done it yet. I want to see those as soon as possible."

Ted replied, "I will be back in touch with you about all that. Thank you for coming in, Mr. Carr."

Ted's 10:30 appointment was waiting for him, and he handled that, which did not take much time. Then he called Rod Olson and asked if he could come to Ted's office. Rod came with a figurative question mark on his face. "Take a look at this, Rod," Ted said. "Jesse Carr has just paid me an 'urgent' visit, and he virtually threw this document across my desk at me, saying that his brother - my client - wants him to be Mr. Carr's 'power of attorney' - he means attorney-in-fact, of course, the holder of the power, and it looks like Rand Carr is named as his alternate, although you could read it to mean that Rand is a co-holder of the power. It's obvious what has happened. Jesse and Rand went to Mr. Carr and told him they knew he needed help now that John was gone, and they wanted to help him, but they needed him to sign this document so they could do it, and so that everyone would know he approved. In his present state of mind, I am sure he feels isolated and misses John, and he either does not remember his estrangement from Jesse, or he feels he doesn't want to offend Jesse because he might need him. I am confident he never had any idea that he was replacing me when he signed this, nor did he otherwise understand what the document says. I know for a fact his eyesight would not permit him to read it. Trustingly, he just signed whatever they put in front of him, thinking it would give him an extra level of protection. I am still the Trustee and potential Executor under the will, but of course, those will be the next two documents they will change. The question is, what do I do with this document? Do I accept it at face value and be glad it liberates me from the morass of family problems I would inevitably have to deal with? A person has a right to change his mind, you know."

Rod looked at the document with disbelief. "Ted, didn't you just meet with Mr. Carr two days ago to help Rand with a financial request, and he didn't mention to you that he would be replacing you?"

"That's right," Ted said. "Never a word about this, and, of course, the Mr. Carr I have known all these years would have mentioned it if he had had any such thing in mind. After a quarter of a century relationship, he would have done me the courtesy of saying something like, 'Ted, I have been thinking it over, and I think I need to make a change," something like that. But he treated me with trust and fully recognized me as his attorney-in-fact when I visited with him two days ago. No hint she was thinking of a change."

"And of course. Rand was with you. He must have known he was going to be somewhere in the mix of the new power of attorney, and he didn't mention it either, I gather," Rod remarked.

"Obviously, Rod, Rand was directly involved. He knew all about it and might well have recruited his uncle to play the key role. No, Rand didn't mention it, because he wanted to get the loan from his Dad, and he thought my involvement would help him get it. So, he saw to it that no word of the coup would come out until after he got the money. Once he got it, Jesse was unleashed to come into my office and deliver the bombshell. And to think: I went out of my way to help Rand, when he really needed help, and I was not even sure I had authority to do it, nor that Mr. Carr was competent to do it, but I felt he would have done it had he been competent. Just goes to show, no good deed goes unpunished."

"The question remains," Rod observed, "what do we do with this so-called power of attorney?"

"I need to think about it, Rod, and I need your input.

Easy thing would be just to turn it all over to Jesse and Rand. I could do that, you know. I'd be rid of a can of worms, dealing with this family, where I see nothing but trouble down the road. I could rationalize it, just say to myself, 'the law presumes the signer of a document is competent to sign it' and 'everyone has a right to change his or her mind.' Therefore, I could just walk away and focus on my other clients, of which I have plenty, and live happily ever after. I could do that, and nobody could criticize me, and I would avoid the inevitable charge that I was trying to hang on to get fees. You know, we've never made any great amount of money on any of the work for Mr. Carr. We have been honored to do the work for a fine and outstanding person, but our fees have been minimal compared to other clients, because the Carr work has usually taken less time than most of my other projects – and I was just going to charge regular hourly fees to handle this, a decent fee but nothing to brag about, and likely not worth the headache. There is just one thing that bothers me."

"What's that?" Rod asked.

"Jesse Carr. If Mr. Carr had named anyone else in the world as his replacement attorney-in-fact, I would lean heavily toward accepting it and letting it go, get on with my life. But Jesse - Jesse is different. He is the one person in the world, he told me time after time over many years, that he never wanted to have anything to do with his financial affairs. Not only that, but he extracted a commitment from me that I would never let that happen. Naively, I vowed to him I never would let it happen. Mainly, at the time I made the commitment, I was in my forties, and I was not as conscious of how estate planning could be undone due to the problems of aging and the mental and physical declines that go with it. I did not factor in the possibility that Mr. Carr, with his adamant feelings about his brother Jesse, might be induced in his infirmities to take actions to undo all his careful planning. I shouldn't have made that vow, because it was never something solely within my power to uphold. But I made it, and he trusted me to carry through. At this point, I have suspicions about his competency, but he has never been examined by a professional, and I can't be sure of it. Yes, he is 93 years old, but not everybody that age is incompetent to execute legal documents that are volitional. There are no plain and simple answers or solutions. I've got to think about this."

"One thing about this, Ted, is that Mr. Carr could scarcely blame you doing what his own signature says he wants you to do TODAY, not some direction he gave to you years ago. Let's say your client Mr. Carr had passed away, and somehow Jesse got himself - or tried to get himself - appointed to a position involving the disposition of his assets. In that case, Mr. Carr would not be here to defend himself or speak for himself, and your 'vow' would come into play. I think you would have at least a moral obligation to defend against that. But he hasn't gone away. He is still here. He can speak for himself, and he arguably has spoken. Wouldn't you be fighting against him, or it would at least have that appearance, if you contested the new power of attorney?" Rod argued.

"But is he really here, Rod?" Ted asked rhetorically. "Is the man who sits all day in that sitting room, blind, arthritic, probably diabetic, mentally diminished - is he the same person with the same mind that has been my client all these years, and who looked to me to protect his interests? Maybe he is *not* really here to defend himself. In that case, do I have a moral, and perhaps a legal, obligation to do what he has always counted on me to do?"

"Then it all comes down to his mental competency," said Rod. "But that raises yet another question. If the only way to 'protect his interests' is to embarrass him and perhaps despoil his memory and the public's perception of him in the twilight of his life, by attacking his mental faculties, is it worth it? And is this what he would want you to do if he were right here in the room with us, rationally discussing this situation?"

"I can't answer that for sure, Rod, but I know Alexander Carr has been a fighter, a feisty person, who would never tolerate anyone taking advantage of him. I think he would want his true intentions carried out, whatever the cost, but of course I can't be sure of that. If anyone asked him that question now, he might give a different answer, and I feel sure his extended family would say it would be unthinkable to sully his reputation by questioning his competency. It is definitely an important consideration, but I can't say it disposes of the ultimate question of what we do."

"Let's sleep on it. We don't have to decide it today," said Rod.

"One thing we do need to decide quickly, perhaps not today, but very soon, is whether we give Jesse a copy of the Trust and Mr. Carr's last will. Before he got Mr. Carr to sign this new power of attorney, he had no real standing to demand copies of those documents, as we were not at liberty to provide him the copies without the client's consent. But now that he has this piece of paper purportedly giving him the power to act on behalf of the client, it will be much harder to refuse him. We could take the position that the 'new' power of attorney is not valid, but what if we are wrong? What if some court eventually says it was valid and we have dishonored it? We could have some liability. Of course, we know what is going to happen if we turn over the documents to them: Jesse will take them and re-write them, just putting his and Rand's names in place of mine, and that will complete his takeover of Mr. Carr's financial affairs - the very opposite of what Mr. Carr wanted, and all ironically based on his own signatures," Ted said, thinking ahead.

"It's complicated, all right. Let's think hard, and fast. We have to make some decisions soon." Rod concurred.

CHAPTER NINE

THE PARTIES MEET IN COURT

Ted and Rod reconvened to talk through the options for dealing with Jesse's power of attorney document. "Rod, I've been thinking about this problem, actually praying about it, didn't get much sleep last night. Here's what I'm thinking we ought to do - and check me if I've overlooked something or am not thinking right about it. As things stand now, we can't definitively say whether this new power of attorney document is valid or not, because it hinges on competency and undue influence, and that has not been determined authoritatively, even though we have our doubts, and our doubts are reasonable, I think. It would be as wrong for us, based on our knowledge, to walk away and let an injustice be done, honoring a spurious document, as it would be to dishonor the document which conceivably might be upheld as a valid power of attorney. Therefore, we are caught in the middle, torn between our obligation to our client, on the one hand, not to honor a possibly spurious document, and our obligation to respect this document if it is indeed valid and reflects Mr. Carr's current rational judgment. Why don't we just do this? Let's file a motion with the Probate Court, laying out all the facts as we know them, and state that we are not able to determine the validity of the new power of attorney document, and ask the Court for instructions as to whether we should honor it or not? Presumably, the Court will set the motion for a hearing within 30 to 40 days, hopefully, and will decide whether to call witnesses. We will not say that Mr. Carr is mentally incompetent, only that the validity of the document cannot be determined and ask the Court to instruct us as to whether it should be honored. If the Court says the new power of attorney is valid, then we will have a judicial determination backing it up, and we would be entirely justified in accepting that. In other words, we will have sought judicial oversight and we will have been justifiably guided by that in accepting the validity of the new power. On the other hand, if the Court says the new power is *not* valid then we will have a judicial determination protecting us in our continued performance of our duties as they existed before we were handed the new document, and all the banks, brokerage firms and others would likewise be assured they can deal with us as the true custodians of Mr. Carr's financial affairs. How does that sound?"

"Sounds pretty good to me," said Rod, "but clarify something for me: How do we avoid alleging Mr. Carr's incompetency?"

"We just say we don't know, but we are asking the Court to determine that and any other issues pertinent to a decision, such as undue influence," Born replied.

"OK, I'm satisfied," said Rod. "I'll draft a motion and you can review it, and then we will file it and see what happens. I take it you are willing to accept the Court's determination, whatever it might be?"

"That's right, absolutely. I would shed no tears over it if the Court simply says, 'Hearing no evidence of Mr. Carr's incompetency, I find that the new power of attorney is valid.' At least the facts as we know them have been called to the Court's attention and the Court will have made a decision. We would not be particularly advocating one decision over another."

The Motion for Instructions was filed, and it was predictably opposed by Jesse Carr and, at least nominally, all his children. There had been a convocation of the Carr relatives at which the figurative podium was occupied mainly by Jesse and Rand Carr, arguing that Born was an outsider who had no business controlling Carr family financial affairs, and he would be getting a big fat fee that would come out of the pockets of everyone present. Rand said the attorney who drafted Jesse's power of attorney would appear at the court hearing on behalf of the family. It was emphasized that the family should present a united front against outsider Born, notwithstanding the fact that some of them had reservations about Uncle Jesse who, to a considerable extent, had up to now been something of an outsider to both the John and Zander Carr sides of the family. Jesse had a vindictive side, perhaps egged on by his strident wife Candace, whom hardly any of Zander's progeny warmed up to. But, in the interest of family harmony and solidarity, no one was prepared to break ranks in support of Ted Born, who was mostly an unknown quantity to all of them.

A court hearing was set and Born and Olson approached the hearing with the hope that it would be the one and only hearing on the controversy, but recognizing that anything was possible. Born, speaking for his side, laid out the background of his decades-long representation of Alexander Carr, his request that Born serve as his alternate executor and continuing over a number of subsequent versions of the will as it was revised from time to time, as recently as two years earlier. He noted that, when Mr. Carr in more recent years set up a living Trust, he again asked Ted to be his alternate at that time as well, and that he was additionally the alternate power of attorney holder. Born told of Mr. Carr's repeated instructions to him that Jesse Carr must never have anything to do with his financial affairs. Mr. Carr was now 93 years old, had severe macular degeneration to the point of blindness, as well as arthritis, and possibly other ailments and had been under emotional distress at the loss of his favorite brother John. Ted related how he had been confronted with the surprise new power of attorney without any mention by Mr. Carr that he had such a change under consideration. All this had raised a question in Born's mind as to whether the new power of attorney had been executed knowingly and of Mr. Carr's own volition. He mentioned he had been excluded from personally inquiring of Mr. Carr what his intentions were, being denied access at the direction of Jesse Carr, so Born understood. Born concluded by saying that he came not so much as an advocate but as someone caught in a dilemma as to his duty to his long-time client and the facial import of this new and inconsistent power of attorney paper whose provenance he did not know. He came seeking the Court's instructions and guidance, and he would accept the Court's decision whatever it might be.

Greg Tween, Rand's golfing friend attorney, speaking, as he said, for the family, emphasized that everyone was presumed competent to execute the documents they signed in the absence of proof to the contrary, of which there had been none presented. He argued that people have a right to change their minds, and that there was ample reason for Mr. Carr to choose his only surviving brother over a non-family member. He also denied there had been any estrangement, just the occasional differences common to all families. He urged the Court to find the new power of attorney to be valid.

Probate Judge Justin Holcomb, presiding at the hearing, indicated that he was not prepared to render a decision based on what he had heard that day, but that the parties should get prepared to come back for a further hearing with sworn testimony. Born took some comfort in that the Judge had listened intently to his presentation and that the Judge at least had resisted the temptation to take the easy way out by just ruling for Jesse's side based on a presumption of competence. Perhaps more importantly, he entered an order that, pending a final ruling in the case, Born would continue to serve as Trustee of the Living Trust for Alexander Carr, but allowing Jesse Carr to handle his regular bank account and other household and personal matters. Despite some positive indication that Judge Holcomb was listening to Born's arguments, it appeared there would be no quick resolution of the matter that would resolve the whole matter.

Jesse and the family members who had been at the hearing, left the courthouse and went to the office of their lawyer Greg Tween to assess what had happened at the hearing. Jesse was outspoken: "I don't think I like what I heard this morning. There wasn't a bit of evidence that Zander was incapable of making up his mind and signing my power of attorney, but still that Judge looks like he is going to drag things out, and God knows what or when we'll get a decision in our favor. Even worse, he's going to let that Born guy continue as Zander's Trustee until we get everything worked out. Hell, that's where most of Zander's money is - in that Trust! And the Judge is going to let Born continue to control all that money for a while, maybe for as long as it takes to try this case. Greg, how long is this confusing and unworkable situation going to continue?"

"Hard to say," Greg answered. "Probate Judges have so many administrative responsibilities, and there are always so many estates going through probate, they don't move very fast. We will do what we can to speed things up, but we can't control that. You need to consider, too, that these proceedings could very well involve Zander. He might have to give a deposition or come down to the courthouse for hearings, and you should think about whether you want to put him through all that. Seems to me, in the interest of getting things resolved quickly, and protecting Zander from getting entangled in all this, we ought to think about some sort of compromise."

"What kind of compromise do you have in mind? Seems to me, either we win or Born wins, so how could we compromise?" Jesse asked.

"Well, the most obvious approach I can think of would be for you and Born to work together jointly. You could agree to be co-trustees, co-holders of the power of attorney, and in case of his death, you could be co-executors.

I know Ted Born. He is a reasonable guy, and I think you would find you could work with him," Tween offered.

"Dammit, Greg! Whose side are you on? Zander signed the papers. He wants ME to make the decisions. If you get that gold-digging lawyer in the mix, I can imagine what's going to happen: He's going to run up his legal fees, for one thing, so we wouldn't have accomplished a damned thing in terms of cost savings. And I don't want to have to go running to him every time I need to make a decision. He could be an obstructionist, and then, what do we do? We've burned our bridges behind us - we will have signed an agreement to let him be a co-something, and then we are stuck with it. If you think about it, you just know damn well something like that is not going to work. And it would be an injustice to Rand, because, if anyone else is entitled to be involved in the decisions, it should be Rand, as he's named in the power of attorney. Can't just ignore that." Jesse obviously was in no mood to compromise.

Rand spoke up, "I'm not so worried about whether I am directly involved or not. I just think a family member should do it, not some outside lawyer like Born. But Jesse is our uncle and Dad's brother, and he is the logical one to do it, and he is taking his responsibility very seriously, as he should. I think we need to be pro-active and not sit around and just see how long it takes for things to wend their way through the Probate Court."

Jesse interjected, "Greg, is there something you can do to take the fight to Born? Looks to me like we have a good argument that he is just in this for a big fee, maybe a million dollars. Isn't that a betrayal of a client? Can't we confront him and get him disqualified or something, accuse him of unethical conduct?"

"I don't think I could go that far, Jesse. He has represented Zander for a long, long time, and it would be hard for us to argue that Zander wasn't aware of what he was doing when he named Born as his alternate. Besides, Born is pretty well known in the bar and among the Judges. It could boomerang against us if we came on too strong with personal attacks." Greg counseled. "I don't think I could do that, and I don't think it would be wise from your standpoint, either."

The other family members were mostly silent and passive, present mainly to find out what was going on, but looking to Jesse and Rand, and Greg Tweet, for advice. Kate said little, but she wondered if the family members had gotten themselves into something that would come to no good end by trying to displace Born.

Greg suggested everyone go home and think about it, then get back and discuss it further. "Would you like me to telephone Born and see if he would be amenable to a joint approach, like I mentioned? At least we could find out if that might be an option."

Rand spoke up and said, "In my opinion, I don't think you should make that call, Greg, at least not yet. Our objective is still to get rid of Born. He seems to be a domineering type of guy and, being a lawyer, he would try to run all over the rest of us. Let's break up for now, and plan to reconvene in a few days." The meeting broke up, but, as they left Greg's office, Jesse gathered his relatives together in a corner of the parking lot and said, "I know Greg is a good friend of Rand's, and I know he's a specialist in this kind of case. But I get the feeling he's too laid back, too respectful of Born, - not the kind of aggressive and activist lawyer we need in this situation. Let's ask around and maybe interview a few people and see what we can come up with as an alternative. Is that all right with the group?" Kate ventured the opinion that this all might not end well, that maybe they should consider a compromise. But Jesse was strongly opposed, and she let the idea drop at that point. The family members all departed in their respective cars.

Rand lost no time calling up lawyers that he knew and trying to get opinions as to which ones were the toughest and most aggressive in probate practice. One name kept coming up: Mona Shadduck. He was told that her real name was Desdemona, named after the character from Shakespeare's "Othello," but commonly uses the shortened form "Mona." He called her and set up a meeting. Rand explained what had transpired and where matters stood at this point. Mona commented, "I don't really know Ted Born because I specialize in probate work, and I never run into him in the Probate Court. I think he mainly litigates in the Federal Courts or does corporate work. I know he is considered one of the so-called senior members of the bar, been around a long time. Don't know anything bad about him. But sometimes good senior lawyers let the lure of money get to them and they get themselves in a conflict of interest. I don't mind taking him on; I think I can make him beg to get out of this case."

"One thing you should know, Mona," Rand advised, "is that there is a question whether Dad has got some dementia. We would like to stay away from that for two reasons. First, we don't want to embarrass him or have to put him through the ordeal of having to get on the witness stand. Second, and quite frankly, I don't know what he might say if he was put on the stand. So, we would want you to try to avoid that, if possible."

"I'll try, Rand," Mona responded. "I'll try to make things so hot and miserable for Ted Born that he will drop out before we ever get to that point, maybe even get him to pay money in order to get out. But I can't make any guarantees. These cases sometimes have a life of their own, and you can't control everything. My strategy would be to make Ted Born the focus of this case, the principal defendant in this case. We'll sue him and get his legal malpractice carrier involved. They will probably pressure him to get out. Maybe his law firm will also put pressure on him to get out. That's the way to win this kind of case. You'll see. I've got the guts to take him on. One important question: can you pay my fees, with Born controlling the Trust?"

"I don't think your payment is a problem. Dad has a lot of liquid assets that are not in the Trust, and the house is not in the Trust. If we have to, we could even mortgage the house," Rand said.

"Well, I would want a large upfront nonrefundable retainer to get into this, and I would want to be sure those upfront fees get replenished as we go along. Those are my terms, not negotiable." Mona seemed very firm.

Rand advised that he would need to talk with his Uncle Jesse and other family members first, but he would be in touch again shortly.

CHAPTER TEN

A TARGET ON BORN'S BACK

G reg Tween called Ted Born, "Hi, Ted. Greg Tween here. Just wanted to let you know, as a courtesy, I'm out of the Carr case. Yeah, got a call earlier today from Rand Carr telling me that I am being replaced, with the family's thanks, of course. But I think they want a more aggressive lawyer. I might have made a mistake in counseling that we explore a compromise, which didn't go over well with the Jesse team. And, yeah, they got an aggressive lawyer, all right. She's so aggressive she goes way out of bounds at times. But they've hired her. I thought I would call, didn't want you to be puzzled as to why I suddenly disappeared from the case. Sorry, I think you and I could have worked together to get this crazy situation resolved, but it is not to be. You will be in for a fight."

"Who is this new aggressive lawyer, Greg?" asked Ted.

"I probably shouldn't say anything more, right now. You will be finding out soon, I'm sure. My best."

Ted called his partner Rod, "Rod, I just heard from Greg Tween, who tells me he's being replaced by a 'very aggressive lawyer.' Didn't identify who it was. Must be a woman because he used the word 'she" in referring to the new lawyer. Who could it be?"

"Not sure, Ted. I could think of several. Hope it's not that Mona Shadduck. She has no sense of where the limits are. We'll just have to deal with it when we find out."

Ted and Rod did not have to wait long. Two days later the mail brought them a bundle of papers from Mona Shadduck - three separate motions. In the first one, she moved the Court for an order confirming Ted Born's discharge as attorney-in-fact; a second one sought an emergency hearing; and the third one moved for the dismissal of Born's petition on the ground Born was violating the Bar Association Rules of Professional Conduct by pursuing a claim that would result in irreparable harm to Alexander Carr. Shadduck predictably argued in her motion that everyone is presumed competent to execute documents, that Ted's services as Mr. Carr's "previous attorney" had been terminated, and that a lawsuit seeking a declaration of incompetency would jeopardize his right to control the lawsuit and would put his "good name, reputation, honor, or integrity in issue." The second motion, relating to a request for an emergency hearing, accused Born of tortious interference with Mr. Carr's financial affairs, that Born had appointed himself as Mr. Carr's attorney-in-fact and trustee. The third one suggested that Born's petition for instructions was motivated by a desire on the part of Born's Firm and Born himself to collect fees, saying that Jesse's new power-of-attorney document would save Mr. Carr's beneficiaries "at least $1.8 million in fees and commissions" that Born had "conveniently orchestrated" for himself and his firm.

Ted and Rod got together again to discuss this development, Ted remarked, "Rod, you made a good guess that the new lawyer would be Shadduck. Of course, I don't know her and, to my knowledge have never met her, and she's never met me. You also correctly pegged her as someone who would go out of bounds in her handling of the case. In more than 40 years of practicing law, including being head of the bar Grievance Committee, no one has ever accused me of putting my own interests ahead of my client's, or doing anything else unethical. It's all a matter of record, what I've done. I never even asked the Court to resolve this matter in my favor; I only asked the Court to exercise appropriate oversight because this sudden new power of attorney was so inconsistent with a quarter of a century of Mr. Carr's estate planning and was done during a period when he was elderly and had a lot of health issues. I even told the Court at the first hearing that I would accept whatever ruling the Court would make and would gladly walk away if the Court found Mr. Carr intended to put Jesse in charge. These new Shadduck motions really irritate me!"

Rod nodded. "I know. It's too bad lawyers are allowed to file stuff like this, impugning the reputation of someone like you. You can see her strategy, though. She is trying to -"

"I know," Ted interrupted. "She is trying to make me the defendant, and shift attention away from Jesse's misconduct in procuring Mr. Carr's signature on the power of attorney, almost certainly without Mr. Carr's understanding of what he was signing. Shadduck's trying to put pressure on me to drop the case. She is threatening both me and the Firm with personal liability if we continue. And it does two other things. First, we will be required to report to our malpractice insurance carriers that I have been sued and the Firm has been named also as being complicit in my actions. The Firm obviously does not like for its lawyers to get sued, and Mona Shadduck knows that this might result in the Firm's putting pressure on me to drop the case. The other thing her motions accomplish is effectively to limit me and our Firm from leading the litigation in the case. You know the old saying, 'a lawyer who defends himself has a fool for a client.' We can still be attorneys of record, but we will have to get someone else to take the lead in defending us in depositions and

Court appearances. Of course, we can still ghostwrite briefs and motions, or most of them, but someone else will need to take the depositions and appear in Court on our behalf. This increases the costs on our side and complicates the communications and coordination aspects. It's all unfortunate and a great disservice to Mr. Carr, but we will just have to deal with it."

"Well, I'm sure the Firm won't be happy about this," observed Rod, "and unfortunately there will be some who, not knowing all the facts, will just say, 'let's get rid of this lawsuit. It's not worth it to jeopardize the Firm and maybe increase our malpractice premiums and maybe result in bad publicity for the Firm'. That's the business side of the matter."

"But the business side is not everything. I made a vow to Mr. Carr, and he trusted and depended on me, and now I find myself called on to honor that vow. We are members of a profession where we have to put the client's interests first. I don't see how I can do otherwise," Ted countered.

"I understand her real name is Desdemona, from the somewhat wild and disobedient - and tragic - daughter in Shakespeare's 'Othello.' But usually she identifies herself as 'Mona,' which is shorter but still unflattering in translation from Spanish. Still, by whatever name, we have no choice but to deal with her lack of boundaries and judgment, which make her both tragic and dangerous."

The Probate Judge scheduled a further hearing, but he did not confirm the discharge of Ted Born or his Firm. He simply set some target dates for completion of discovery, looking toward an eventual trial. Mona Shadduck was not happy about that, and she called a meeting with the Carr family members. "Well, I think we have them on the run. They're playing defense now, but it looks like the Probate Judge is not being as receptive to our arguments as we had hoped, and so far he isn't buying the picture we are trying to paint. I don't think he's going to do anything to change the status quo until we get to a trial in this case, and I'm trying to force the issues before we get to that point. We are going to have to let a psychiatrist or psychologist, appointed by Born, examine Zander. We don't know what will come out of that, but there's a good chance Born will choose someone who will find the way Born wants him to find, and that could give some encouragement to his side. Obviously, that's not what we want. We want to smash Born and his case right now and get this whole thing behind us."

"How do we do that, Mona?" asked Jesse.

"Okay. I have a plan. It might seem crazy. It might sound like we are just complicating things but hear me out. We can go to another Court. You've probably never heard of something called 'concurrent jurisdiction,' but what that means it that more than one Court can have jurisdiction of the same case at the same time. So, the Probate Court has jurisdiction, but at the same time our

Circuit Court also can exercise jurisdiction, just like the Probate Court. But we have to move quickly because a case in Circuit Court has to be filed before a 'responsive pleading' is filed in the Probate Court – which hasn't happened yet but will happen shortly. We've been dealing with motions up to now, but a responsive pleading means filing an answer, and we haven't gotten there yet in the Probate Court, fortunately. Now, the good thing is that the Circuit Court moves a lot faster than the Probate Court. Whichever case goes to trial first is the only one that counts, and the other one becomes moot, at least as to the common issues. If we initiate a new case in the Circuit Court, there is a good chance that the new case would move faster and get us to trial before the Probate case. If we are lucky and draw a Circuit Judge that seems more favorable to us than the Probate Judge, this would increase the pressure on Born to get out. Hopefully, we would never have to go to trial in either case, but the fear of a Circuit Court trial might force Born to drop his claims."

"Is this going to cost more money, Mona?" asked Rand.

"Yes, it will cost more, but not a lot more, because all the depositions and other discovery we do in one case could still be used in the other case; we wouldn't have to do duplicate work. And most of the pleadings are going to be similar. The main thing is, it gives us another option to put pressure on Born," Shadduck answered.

"Then, I'm game to try it," said Rand. "Do we all agree?"

Kate spoke up, "So far, we just have a confusing mess, which is what I was afraid of. I'm not that encouraged, but we've gone this far, and I guess we don't have a lot of choice but to take this step, but this is about as far as I want to go. And it seems to me that instead of saving money that would be going to lawyers instead of to us, we might end up paying even more legal fees to two or three sets of lawyers. Litigation is expensive, as we all know." Two of the brothers seemed largely in agreement with Kate. Yet, while not enthusiastic, they were willing to acquiesce to Uncle Jesse.

Mona added, "It is very important for the Carr family to present a unified front when we go into the Circuit Court. If all of you, who of course know your Dad best, believe he is mentally competent and you are in favor of your Uncle Jesse's being in charge, that will go a long way with the Judge, especially given the presumption of competence which the law implies, and there being no contrary evidence. What we need is an affidavit from each of you stating that you believe your Dad is of sound mind, that you believe he was fully mentally competent to execute the power of attorney in favor of your Uncle Jesse, and that you believe Jesse is his legal attorney-in-fact and you have confidence in his handling of your Dad's affairs. I have affidavits ready for each of you individually to sign, which I will give you now. I would like you to read them and let's get them signed if you agree," announced Mona. "I also plan to get an affidavit from your Dad's regular Doctor, and maybe from others attesting to his mental capacity."

The Carr siblings took the affidavits and read them, then looked at Mona, and then at each other. Then they looked at their Uncle Jesse who was staring at them. Rand volunteered to sign his affidavit. One of the others said he was not really comfortable with it but would go ahead and sign. Kate then said, "I hate to say it, but I really do have questions about Dad's state of mind. I'll need to think about this, and I would need to go over it with Jason Smith, our family attorney, before signing it."

"Well, I know you all want to be loyal to your Uncle Jesse, but if you need a little time, I can give you a couple of days, but we need to get this case filed in the Circuit Court as soon as we can, and these affidavits are important." Mona said. Still, Kate and Bruce said they wanted the extra time.

The Circuit Court case was filed shortly thereafter, with supporting affidavits by all the Carr family members. Ted Born was served with the several documents in the filing, including the family affidavits. He noticed that all the affidavits were identical in wording, except for Kate's. Hers was a watered-down version which skirted the competency issue, just saying that Alexander signed the papers and that she was in favor of Jesse's serving as the attorney-in-fact.

Meanwhile, the Executive Committee of Ted's Firm was meeting, and the Chairman advised the members of the complaint that a suit had been filed against Born, possibly implicating the Firm as well. "We have this Complaint that has been filed against Ted Born, claiming that he is resisting a power of attorney and revisions to other estate planning documents that his wealthy client has signed, replacing him in certain fiduciary capacities. They say he's trying to hang on to get some fees for himself and for the Firm and he is interfering with his now 'former client' to frustrate his intentions. They are claiming compensatory and punitive damages for this conduct on several different grounds. It looks like Ted has gotten himself in opposition to the whole Carr family, who, as you know is one of the most prominent families around - not good PR for us as a Firm. All the Carr family members are against Ted and in favor of their Uncle Jesse. It is particularly troubling that Ted seems to be bringing into question the mental capacity of his own client, or former client, which also looks unseemly, if not ethically questionable. I've reported it to our malpractice insurer, and it's on their radar screen. Anybody have any suggestions of what, if anything, we should do about this?"

Various members spoke up. Most of them knew Ted very well, and indeed he himself had served for six years on the Firm's Executive Committee. He was a highly compensated partner and well respected for his recognitions and accomplishments. But there were others serving on the Committee who had come into the Firm through mergers, and they did not know Ted so well. Those who knew him expressed the view that Ted must have good reasons for his actions and felt the Firm should back him. Others wondered if the Firm ought to be getting itself into a position that was problematical, in that the net benefits to the firm might well be outweighed by the risks of a case that could be hard to win and could be a PR nightmare. It was agreed that Ted should be told to look for a way to settle or extricate himself from the case at some appropriate time. They did not want to order Ted to drop it immediately when the timing might not be best, but the Firm really would like for him to get out as soon and as favorably as possible - no immediate pressure, but the Firm wanted "out."

The Executive Committee message was delivered to Born. Born explained that the accusations against him were groundless, that he had simply asked the Probate Court for instructions as to handle a situation where an abrupt change had occurred that was totally inconsistent with a quarter century history of Alexander Carr's estate planning. He also said that there was some discovery coming up that would likely position the case for a more favorable settlement than to try to get out right now. He stated that he wanted to resolve the case as badly as anyone, but it would not be wise to rush a settlement.

The Executive Committee agreed to be patient, but they would continue to keep tabs on the progress. Ted thought to himself, "Mona's strategy is beginning to pay dividends, having the desired effect of bringing pressure on me from within my own Firm."

In the meantime, Born had hired a team of outside lawyers to represent him in discovery and in certain courtroom appearances, including Luke Green, a well-respected trial lawyer and past President of the bar association, assisted by a probate law specialist Barry Goodloe, a former Federal Judge H. T. Gideon, and Matilda ("Tilly") Cole, an accomplished up-and-coming trial lawyer. They would be challenged.

CHAPTER ELEVEN

THE CIRCUIT COURT TAKES A LOOK

The first hearing before the Circuit Judge came up quickly. Judge Ephraim Tryon had gotten the assignment for this case and was presiding. Judge Tryon was an African American who had primarily practiced employment law before being elected to the bench by the General Assembly. Ted had met him casually at Bar Association meetings and a few social gatherings while they were both practicing attorneys, but they had practiced in entirely different areas of the law and had never been involved in any litigation together. "All right, I will hear from the plaintiffs first, the family members of Alexander Carr," the Judge said.

Mona Shadduck moved to the podium, and she explained that her clients had filed this lawsuit in the Circuit

Court because they urgently needed a resolution of the issues due to the divided responsibilities of the contested attorneys-in-fact which was confusing in the conduct of Mr. Carr's business and management of his household affairs, and the Probate Court appeared to be moving slowly. So, the Carrs meant no criticism of the Probate Court, Shadduck said, but she knew things just necessarily move more slowly there and so she had invoked the concurrent jurisdiction of the Circuit Court.

"As the Court may know, Alexander Carr is a well-known and generous philanthropist who recently sustained the loss of one of his two brothers who held his power of attorney and was Trustee of a living trust he had made, as well as being designated potentially to serve as his Executor if he survived Alexander. After the brother's death, Alexander decided he wanted his other brother to take over these responsibilities, and he executed a power of attorney in favor of him, Jesse Carr, to do just that. Every member of the Carr family, being his children and next of kin, recognizes that Mr. Carr was competent to make this decision and they have filed affidavits supporting it. However, the earlier papers had listed his lawyer as an alternate, sort of a stand-in 'just in case' situation - Mr. Ted Born - and our problem is that he refuses to recognize what his former client has done (he's replaced Mr. Born now as his attorney), but Mr. Born is fighting to hold on, as a former alternate, so that he can manage Mr. Carr's money and get a huge fee. Now, Mr. Carr is 93 years old, and he has always been a good manager of his financial affairs, but he has some underlying problems now, like macular degeneration, that causes him to need some help. His mind is sound, and he has made the perfectly logical choice that he needs a family member, a brother he has grown up with and who knows him intimately - not a lawyer consumed in his law practice who will act like an absentee landlord.

"He needs a family member who will come by and see him every day, check on him, take him to the doctor and see that his household is managed for his benefit. He has made this logical and compelling choice, which is clearly in his interest, and will save him tons of money besides, because his brother Jesse will not charge anything for his services. But Ted Born is holding on like a bulldog, and it is embarrassing to Mr. Carr, suggesting he is not competent to make this obvious decision. This is not the legacy that Mr. Carr deserves, to have it spread all over the newspapers and media that he is accused of being incompetent. But it appears Mr. Born will stop at nothing to thwart his former client's decision. This is a shameful thing, and he deserves to be held fully accountable for it in compensatory and punitive damages. Instead of being supportive of his now *former* client, he has chosen to go to war against him."

"Unfortunately," Shadduck continued, "the status of the matter, as it stands in the Probate Court, is that Born holds the purse-strings of Mr. Carr's Trust until this case is finally disposed of, which is where most of his assets are, while his brother Jesse has the day-to-day respon-sibility for his brother's well-being and has much more limited resources for doing that. I would point out that I represent the entire family, all the near kin of Mr. Carr, his brother Jesse and every single one of his children who are all united, of one accord, in supporting the claims that have been filed against Mr. Born on behalf of Mr. Carr. You can see, Your Honor, that this is an urgent matter, and it needs and deserves a quick resolution, which is why we are here before your Court today. We are hopeful this Court can help." Shadduck sat down.

"What say the defendants?" asked the Judge, looking toward the table where Born's lawyers were seated.

"May it please the Court," said former Judge H. T. Gideon, who, like Judge Tryon was African American, "it will be no surprise to Your Honor to hear that we have a quite different view of this case. Mr. Born has rep-resented Mr. Carr for some 25 years during which time there was a relationship of complete trust between them, and he named Ted born as his alternate Executor not just once, but in TWELVE different iterations of Mr. Carr's will, to say nothing of all the codicils along the way, and when he set up his living trust, he named Mr. Born as his alternate in that document, and likewise he has named him as his alternate in each of his powers of attorney. During all this time, he COULD have named his brother Jesse as his alternate. But he deliberately chose *not* to do that. He had named his other brother John Carr, now deceased, as his primary representative in all these documents, but he made the deliberate choice not to include the other brother Jesse in any role whatsoever in his estate planning - over a period of nearly a quarter of a century, when no one doubts he was astute and capable. Now why would he have included one brother and excluded the other one? The answer is, he was estranged from brother Jesse for all those years, rarely speaking to each other, and giving explicit instructions – "

Shadduck was on her feet objecting, "I object, Your Honor. This is sheer speculation. There is no evidence of estrangement. We expect the evidence to show that Mr. Born took it on himself to put his own name in those documents. The Court will recognize that even astute people like Mr. Carr either don't read long and complicated wills word-for-word or in any case they don't pay much attention to or attach much significance to alternates, because their focus is on the primary person. We ask the Court to disregard the speculation as to why Jesse Carr was not named in the earlier documents. The important thing is what he has most recently done."

Mr. Gideon responded: "There is no admissible evidence before the Court about any of this, no evidence YET of what we are saying nor of what Ms. Shadduck is saying, and we think there will *never* be evidence of the critical assertions she has made. When the evidence is presented, we expect it to show that Jesse Carr, perhaps with the help of one or more of his nephews, took advantage of a vulnerable Mr. Carr, 93 years old and suffering from a multitude of ailments, essentially blind, hardly mobile from arthritis, a diabetic or at least a pre-diabetic, and suffering also from dementia. We have not yet had an opportunity to have Mr. Carr examined by a professional psychiatrist to assess competency, but we are very certain he suffers from dementia to a significant degree. He was vulnerable, and he was taken advantage of by an envious estranged younger brother, never successful himself, but always envious of his older brother's wealth and eager to get his hands on it. So, he put a piece of paper in front of Mr. Carr and asked him to sign it. In his state, he doubtless would have signed anything, not realizing that this paper could undo all of his careful estate planning of 20-plus years in the making. We want nothing but to see that Mr. Carr's true intent is carried out. If it is determined, after the evidence is in, that Mr. Carr consciously and knowingly made the decision to strike Mr. Born and substitute the name of his brother, then that will be accepted. Mr. Born has never sought anything except the thoughtful oversight of a Court as to whether he should accept or not accept the paper that Mr. Jesse Carr recently got Mr. Alexander Carr to sign."

Ms. Shadduck rose to speak, but the Judge waved her down, saying: "I've heard enough. Here's what we are going to do. First, I am convinced that this is an urgent matter that does need to be resolved as soon as possible. I am not going to interfere with the rulings of the Probate Court that Mr. Born should continue to serve as Trustee pending the final disposition of this matter. But I believe we should proceed to trial as soon as possible. I must say that I am at this point skeptical of the defendant, Mr. Born's arguments. The fact that Mr. Carr has some infirmities and is 93 years old is not convincing to me. My own mother is in her 90's and is just as sharp as ever, and it will take some very strong evidence to convince me that I should ignore the law's presumption that everyone is competent to sign what they have signed until proven otherwise. If we start rejecting signed documents every time someone alleges they were not knowingly executed, the result would be chaos. So, I advise the parties that I view the incompetency argument with considerable skepticism, though I obviously have not heard the evidence yet and have an open mind. But I know that circumstances change, and people's perceptions of their circumstances change, and sometimes they have a change of mind. Years ago, when Mr. Carr was young and healthy and named Mr. Born as his alternate, he likely had no perception of what his true needs would be when he got older and his health had deteriorated, and I can see how he would change his mind and decide he needed a family member to help him make decisions, not a lawyer. That is a very logical decision, makes a lot of sense, and at this point I don't see anything sinister about it. To the contrary, I see it as the need for family coming to the fore in realization of his needs, justifying replacement of Ted Born. Well, we will see what the evidence shows, and I will have an open mind, but I think Mr. Born has his work cut out for him. Let's proceed with discovery as quickly as possible, and I will enter some scheduling orders at the appropriate time." The parties rose from their table, and it was obvious that Mona Shadduck was elated with the outcome of this hearing - a Judge much more receptive to her arguments than the Probate Judge.

Born's group went directly to the office of the defense team. Born spoke first, "Judge Gideon, I thought you did a very fine job of laying out our position in this preliminary encounter in Circuit Court – very pleased with how you handled it. But for some reason we find ourselves in a Court where the Judge has at least an initially negative view of our side, and he appears to be trying to win a race to judgment in competition with the Probate Judge. I think I understand what is happening. Judge Tryon sits on a Court that rarely hears these probate-type conflicts, and his first instinct is to lean on the presumptions he is familiar with, like the presumption that everyone is competent to execute the documents they sign. On the other hand, the Probate Judge has had a lot of experience with situations where some family members will take advantage of elderly and ailing relatives who are vulnerable and are experiencing some dementia. Now, I don't doubt that there are some 93-year-olds that are perfectly competent, mentally and physically, to make considered volitional decisions on estate matters. But when the average person reaches that age *and* has all these underlying conditions, the probabilities change in our favor – and we forgot to mention that we found out he has cardio-vascular problems along with the macular degeneration, arthritis, and maybe diabetes. Just imagine what it must be like to be confined to a sitting room where you cannot read, cannot watch television, have no one to talk to most of the day other than the household staff, no close friends that are real friends, and you know things are not going to get any better. Add to that some dementia, and you have a vulnerable victim who will trust anybody and will do anything he is asked to do. There is a reason why the scam artists concentrate on the elderly; they know older persons are fertile ground for exploitation. The Probate Judges see this pattern, day in and day out, so they are not cowed by the presumption of competency, unlike some Circuit Judges. Of course, we can't be sure what will happen in discovery when we get into our case. Let's start focusing on that."

CHAPTER TWELVE

THE UNSETTLING PROSPECT OF TRIAL

The good news came first. It happened that Judge Holcomb, back in the Probate Court, had just entered a scheduling order relative to discovery, specifying cut-off times for the discovery process, and specifying conditions under which the discovery would be taken. One of them provided for Alexander Carr to be examined by a psychiatrist of Born's choosing, to compare his results with those of the psychologist relied on by Jesse Carr. Born, of course, was working behind the scenes making the strategic decisions within his circle of outside attorneys, even though he was no longer appearing in Court proceedings representing himself. He had had some good prior experience with psychiatric and psychological expert witnesses in past litigations and knew of an excellent neuro-psychiatrist at the University, Dr. William Weinstein, who had done extensive research and writing about dementia issues. Born knew who the opposition's expert was, because Mona Shadduck had recently filed in the Probate Court a conclusory one-page summary from that expert, a psychologist named Dr. Ed Tercelli, concluding that Mr. Carr was, in his opinion, competent to sign legal and testamentary documents. With some difficulty, Born's lawyers had been able to obtain copies of the underlying tests conducted by the psychologist - test results that did not seem to support competency. Born's psychiatrist was not only better qualified, but he also concluded that the test results relied on by Tercelli did not support Tercelli's conclusions. Dr. Weinstein had not yet had an opportunity to examine Mr. Carr. However, his examination of Mr. Carr was about to take place.

When the psychiatric examination by Dr. Weinstein commenced in Mr. Carr's home, he began with a con-versation to get Mr. Carr comfortable and relaxed, and he noted later that, in that initial conversation, he saw the first clear indication of dementia. He said Mr. Carr told him about a painting in his living room, and then repeated the story two more times, with no recollection that he had already told the story once or twice earlier. He gave Mr. Carr a battery of tests where he ranked in the lowest 10 to lowest 25 percentiles on the tests. Despite having once been a recognized leader in finance, he was unable to do simple arithmetic. He could name most of his children, but he left one of them out and could not remember their birth order or their addresses. Some tests could not be completed because his eyesight was so poor. He could not draw a clock and put hour hand numbers on it. All of this was done after Rand Carr and Jesse Carr had met with him in advance of the examination and had discussed with him what he should expect. The neuropsychiatrist was very confident in his conclusion that Mr. Carr in fact was not competent to execute legal documents like powers of attorney, trusts or wills, and he was quite critical of the conclusions reached by the Carr family's proffered psychologist, stating that his broad conclusion of competency was not only *not* supported by the tests he had given, but the test results clearly contradicted those conclusions.

The psychiatric examination was a strong plus for the Born camp, but in itself it did not dispose of the matter. The psychologist still could argue that, despite the poor test scores of Mr. Carr, he still believed Mr. Carr was able to understand and decide to make the decisions reflected in the power of attorney and trust and will documents. But it was a big step forward for Born.

Next, Shadduck took Ted Born's deposition. She adopted a technique of asking him questions over and over with little or no variation in wording, whenever she did not get the answer she wanted. Presumably, she had had luck with other deponents who would expand on their previous answers or even contradict them, and Born's counsel, Luke Green, was nervous that Born might do likewise, based on experience that lawyers can be the worst witnesses of all because they are trained advocates, and they like to hear themselves talk. Born was different. He stuck to his guns, not hard for him. as he told exactly what happened and what he knew, volunteering nothing, but answering the questions fully. The deposition went nowhere, and it was never used in court later.

Meanwhile, the Born team in its discovery was finding some interesting emails between Jesse and Rand and some of the others. The emails provided background information on Jesse's hiring a new CPA – an individual practitioner who was a personal friend of Rand – to displace Mr. Carr's decades-long CPA. Jesse also hired new stockbrokers to sell some of Mr. Carr's individually owned stock, not in the Trust administered by Born. Jesse had engaged in a "cleansing" of everyone Mr. Carr had chosen as his advisers and had substituted those who would be beholden to him and to his instructions and wishes.

There were two emails of special interest obtained by the Born team in discovery. One of them, originating with Jesse, suggested mortgaging Mr. Carr's home to pay the attorney's fees of Mona Shadduck, a startling idea, since Mr. Carr's home had never, ever, had a mortgage on it, and the very idea would have been unthinkable to Zander, even in a state of dementia. Although Rand Carr had previously mentioned to Mona that mortgaging the homeplace might be an option, this was the first concrete evidence Born had found to indicate serious consideration of doing so. Born saw in that email that Jesse was entirely willing to jeopardize his brother Zander's very home in order to try to gain ultimate control over his estate, a gross violation of his fiduciary duty to Mr. Carr, in Born's opinion. The other email was one which suggested that Jesse intended to increase the amount in Zander's will that he was leaving Jesse. The email reflected Jesse concluded it would be a bad idea to make that change amid the ongoing litigation, but he wrote ominously, "There are going to be a whole lot of changes made once we get this litigation behind us!"

One occurrence that caused special concern was that Jesse cooperated with St. Bartholomew's Hospital for Mr. Carr to give it a million dollars, in return for which the hospital would put his name on the front of one of its professional buildings. Of course, Jesse did not have access to that much money, knowing it would have to come out of the Trust that Born was administering. But he had an angle there. While the Trust document would not have permitted Born on his own to commit to such a large charitable gift, there was authorization for making gifts through the Trust *with Mr. Carr's approval.* In a different situation, Mr. Carr had already committed, years earlier, to make an $850,000 gift to the University, and there was still one outstanding payment remaining to be made on that obligation but Born had inherited that commitment and had not been a party to the making of it. A brand-new million-dollar commitment to St. Bartholomew's Hospital was entirely another matter, especially considering Zander's current mental capacity. The million-dollar gift had already been announced in the press. Apparently, Jesse's thinking was that, if Born refused to honor the gift, he would reap horrible publicity, which could hurt Born in the minds of the public, and with charitable entities generally, and it would make him appear to be an obstructionist to Zander's generous philanthropic instincts.

Furthermore, Mr. Carr had been named the Philanthropist of the Year, and there was to be a huge gala celebration at which he would receive this award. If it came out that Born was in a lawsuit with Mr. Carr and that he was also refusing to honor the philanthropist's charitable wishes, it would make Born appear to be mean-spirited in the extreme. As Born considered how to deal with the situation, the hospital fund raiser was openly hostile to Born and was strongly siding with Jesse against Born in the litigation. The fund raiser even filed an affidavit stating his belief that Alexander was competent; he could scarcely have taken any other position if he wanted to get the million-dollar gift for the hospital. He came to see Born, almost threateningly, to get confirmation that Born, as the person at least temporarily in charge of the Trust, would honor the gift. Born told him politely that Mr. Carr's mental competency was a serious issue, and that he had no power under the terms of the Trust to make a gift of that magnitude without Mr. Carr's express permission, which was problematic under the circumstances. He said he would need to consider the issue further before answering. He ultimately concluded to resolve the matter by taking the position he would honor the gift only if all the Carr beneficiaries, under Zander's will, would sign off on it, so that they could not sue him for improperly disposing of Mr. Carr's assets. After all, the money would ultimately be theirs, and they effectively would be giving away a part of their inheritance. Upon getting that written consents, Born advised he would honor the gift and pay the installments as they came due.

Word of these developments got to the Executive Committee of Born's law Firm, and a member of the Committee, Carl Heimat, paid Born a visit to discuss them. "Any progress, Ted, in disposing of the Carr litigation?"

"Well, I think you probably know we got a really good result from our expert witness to the effect that Mr. Carr was not competent to sign the new problematic papers to displace me, and I have survived unscathed the taking of my deposition. We have some very helpful documentary discovery of emails and things, and all this puts us in a much stronger position to get rid of the case. We are not quite there yet, but we are making progress." Born reported.

"That's all good, I guess, although I am sure Mr. Carr's competency will still be contested. Even if you win on that issue, there are still some concerns the Committee has. For one thing, while the competency issue looks like it might be tending favorably to your winning the case, there is concern about winning if it means smearing Mr. Carr's reputation by his own lawyer calling Mr. Carr incompetent. You know, winning can sometimes be losing; you can win a battle and lose the war. Right now, Alexander Carr is riding high in the public's esteem. He's even getting the 'Philanthropist of the Year' Award. What if the Carr family grants an interview with the press, and they praise Mr. Carr and they paint you as a despicable character who is trying to ruin Carr's reputation and is greedily trying to take over his assets and get a big fee? What if they say, 'Ted Born and his Firm are viciously attacking and slandering this grand and generous gentleman?'" Heimat countered.

"Carl, I think the answer is, the Carr family will not take the chance of doing that. First, they know they did wrong. They know, no matter how they try to spin it, that they took advantage of Mr. Carr's dementia to get him to put them in charge, in contradiction to his long-standing estate plans. The evidence is getting stronger and stronger in our favor, and they have every reason to put a lid on that, especially now that we have worked out the gift to St. Bartholomew's." Born put it in perspective, as he saw it.

"What about this Circuit Court case? You think the evidence in your favor is getting stronger, but we understand the hearing before Judge Tryon did not go well.

Does that encourage the Carrs to keep on fighting and put settlement out of reach?" Carl probed.

"You are right that the hearing did not go well, but there was no evidence at the time, and now we have evidence, and the evidence keeps getting stronger. At some point, conditions should come about that will impel the parties to a mutually satisfactory resolution," Born opined.

"What if you are wrong, Ted? It really is not in the Firm's interest for this to go on and on. And this could not only hurt you; it could hurt Rod who is only trying to help you. You wouldn't want that, would you?" Carl asked.

"No, of course I don't want that, Carl. But it seems to me that we are not discussing the right issue. The issue is whether I - and this Firm - have an ethical obligation to a long-time client to honor a commitment made to him years ago and reiterated often thereafter. It was a commitment to do whatever I could to see that Jesse Carr never has anything to do with Mr. Carr's financial affairs. Of course, he temporarily, at least, has control of some of his financial assets, but we are protecting our commitment as best we can. At the time I made that commitment, it was not contrary to any Firm policy or to the policy of any of our malpractice carriers. Even so, I recognize that maybe I should not have made that vow, *but I made it.* I understand that, to honor that commitment, I might have to leave the Firm. In attempting to honor it, I also realize I am subjecting myself and my family to huge liabilities. I am trying to take things one day at a time, believing that in the end, justice will prevail. I have stood by the Firm in tough times before. I hope the Firm will show some patience and stand by me a bit longer."

"I am sure no one wants to do anything precipitous, Ted, and you know I am one of your admirers and supporters, but I just want you to know there are rumblings and you can understand that this is a problem for the Firm, and everyone wants to put problems behind them. Just do the best you can, and let's stay in touch," Carl said.

"Thanks, Carl. I take to heart everything you've said. I'll stay in touch." Ted replied.

At about this point, Rod Olson received an email from Greg Tween, the lawyer who had originally appeared for the other side in the first hearing but who had been displaced. He related how he had encountered the new aggressive lawyer, Mona Shadduck, who told him she had outmaneuvered Born, that there was nothing Born could do about it, and she had the case essentially sewed up. Greg indicated he was neutral and was writing Olson as a favor to warn that if Born continued with the litigation, the result would be the ruin of Born's personal reputation, and he would likely face a huge money judgment leading to his financial ruin. He suggested there might be time to settle the case, but that Born and/or his Firm also might have to agree to pay some money damages, but perhaps of manageable proportions. This email marked a new low point in the case for Born. Greg Tween had addressed and sent it to Born's partner, Rod Olson, rather than to Born, possibly thinking that Born might ignore it if sent to him, but that Rod or other members of the Firm might exert pressure on Born to get out of a very messy, unpleasant and risky case. Born presumed Rod would feel obligated to show the email to members of the Executive Committee, though he had not done so yet.

Born felt alone and isolated in the case. Mr. Carr's family was opposed to him. The Circuit Judge seemed opposed to him, and his own Firm was increasing the pressure on him to walk away from the case. And now, out of the blue, this email came in, purporting to give friendly advice, but coming from a lawyer who had once briefly represented the opposition, telling him he was a loser, but maybe too blind to see that he was a loser. The opposition parties were celebrating their clever strategy of getting a Circuit Judge involved who seemed hostile to Born's case, and it looked like the case would probably be tried in that Court, rather than before the more even-handed Probate Judge.

"Rod, tell me. Am I being foolish, even unfair, to the Carrs, to the Firm, to myself - even to you, who have stood by me all this time? Have I lost my perspective and judgment? Am I expecting too much of our system of justice and should I quit worrying about right and wrong and just cut my losses and walk away? Tell me honestly," Ted asked.

"I don't know, Ted. I have been asking myself that question over and over, and sometimes I think the cost – the toll on our nerves, to say nothing of financial and reputation exposure – just isn't worth it. Here, even Mr. Carr seems against us, and we're doing all this to protect him. And then, when I have these doubts, I remember those meetings we had with Mr. Carr, where he told us repeatedly, and made us promise, that we would never let Jesse have anything to do with his finances. I don't trust Jesse. His willingness to mortgage Mr. Carr's house, and his determination to 'make a whole lot of changes' once the litigation is over - they scare me," Rod answered.

"I wonder, though, Rod, whether I am seeking justice or vindication, and is there a difference? Does justice mean *perfect* justice? Maybe the rest of the Carr family could rein Jesse in and make sure he does not abuse whatever control he gets. Maybe we could just count on the self-interest of the rest of the Carrs to keep him straight. But then, they have docilely sat back and followed his lead, like lemmings headed to the sea, so there's not much sign that they will offer much resistance to him. I need to sleep on it. At this point we haven't been offered any middle way, any compromise, so it looks like our choices are total capitulation or holding out for justice, with maybe some vindication."

Just before leaving the office, Ted got another jolt, a notice that Judge Tryon had set a trial date three months hence. "Damn!" said Ted to himself, who was not given to profanities. "There's no way the Probate Court can match a date set so soon. Looks like fate has given us a rendezvous with - something, God only knows what, in the Circuit Court! Not welcome news."

At home that evening, it was obvious to Lydia that Ted was in low spirits, just wanted to be quiet. "Can you tell me what's up, Ted? I know something's bothering you, must be the Carr case."

"Yeah, I'm afraid it is. Pretty predictable these days, I guess. Rod got an email from Jesse's first lawyer, Greg Tween, who was displaced, but he was saying he ran into his replacement, Mona, and she was in high-spirits that she had out-foxed us by getting the Circuit Court involved, as the Judge she drew turns out to be favorably disposed to her side, at least from initial indications. She is confident there is nothing we can do about it, and that we will inevitably face defeat, loss of reputation and financial ruin. And then the last thing that happened was that I got a notice of a fast-track type trial date from the Circuit Court, guaranteeing that it will be the hostile Judge, and not the more open-minded Probate Judge, who will be presiding over this case. I'm glad I have other cases to help take my mind off this one. I have become the target, the defendant, and the other side is going to try to crucify me. For what? For having the temerity to ask the Probate Court just for instructions! And now I, you, and our family are all at risk," Ted opened up. "You deserve to know that I have put our family at risk, for nothing worse than asking a court to give oversight to a highly suspicious situation, which looks worse and worse the further I get into it."

"There must be a way out, Ted," Lydia said comfortingly. "Doesn't your good name and reputation mean anything? Of all people, no one could believe you ever acted from anything but the best of motives."

"It's not that I ever wanted to do this job, to take charge of Mr. Carr's finances and affairs. I did it as an accommodation that I thought would never happen, and I still don't want the job. But I vowed I would protect Mr. Carr from Jesse, and now Jesse seems to have become his 'new best friend,' and I'm the villain for doing what he asked me to do."

"I'm with you, Ted, for better or for worse, and so is the family, though I don't talk to them much about it. There's got to be a way. I'm sure there's a way." Lydia went back to put dinner on the table. It was a quiet meal, followed by a restless night for Ted.

CHAPTER THIRTEEN

MR. CARR'S DEPOSITION

The trial date set by Circuit Judge Tryon was getting closer. The proximity of the trial at last forced the parties to agree on a deposition date for the testimony of Mr. Carr. It was agreed that the deposition was to take place in his home, as a matter of his convenience. Mr. Carr's deposition was something Ted had pushed for, and that the opposition had put off as long as possible. Yet both sides approached the deposition with apprehension. Jesse and his Carr family allies hoped to find a way to avoid entirely a deposition of Zander, but, having taken the position that Mr. Carr had no dementia and was mentally competent, they could not beg off for medical reasons, nor did they want to give Ted a reason to delay the trial, as they knew no Judge would order the trial to go forward if Jesse's side had blocked the deposition of the key witness whose competency was in issue. Jesse's team had hoped Born would give up the litigation before getting to this point, but that had not happened. Reluctantly, Jesse's counsel recognized the deposition had to take place, and hoped for the best.

On the other hand, Ted was also very nervous about the deposition, because Jesse and the other members of the Carr family for months had had complete control of Mr. Carr and had excluded Ted from any contact with him. Ted assumed they undoubtedly had tried to poison Mr. Carr against him, and there was no way to guess how successful they had been or what he might say. He might perhaps be vitriolic toward Ted. Still, there were a few things that gave Ted hope. There was the long and harmonious twenty-five-year relationship between Ted and Mr. Carr. Then, there was the psychiatrist report that Mr. Carr did indeed have dementia, and Ted thought it likely that the dementia would be evident in the deposition, even if Mr. Carr spoke negatively of Ted. And finally, there was a telephone call that Mr. Carr had initiated a few weeks earlier to Ted for no apparent reason, in which he said he wished Ted would come visit him. Ted had said, "Mr. Carr, if I came to visit you, Jesse would shoot me!" Mr. Carr laughed and replied, "Oh, no, he wouldn't. I would shoot him!" Ted hoped this was an indication that, despite all efforts to turn Mr. Carr against him, his long-time client continued to have positive feelings toward Ted.

Even though Ted was now in a client's status as a defendant and had a team of four other lawyers representing him and taking depositions as their schedules permitted, he had personally prepared outlines and suggested questions to be asked in the depositions, and he always met strategically with the lawyer taking each deposition beforehand, to prepare for it. So, Ted sat down to talk with Luke Green, the lead counsel of the group defending Ted, and the one Ted especially wanted to take the most important deposition in the case, the Alexander Carr deposition. They discussed starting out with soft, friendly questions so that Mr. Carr would think of himself as being engaged in a friendly conversation, rather than in an adversarial interrogation. Luke said he liked to start, preferably in a conversation preceding a key deposition, by establishing some common connection, such as a mutual friend. "That way, the two of us are connected as friends in the deponent's mind through the mutual friend that we share. Is there anybody Zander is close to that I might know?"

"Well," said Ted, "he has a godchild named Sarah Knight, who is about our age. Do you know her?"

"I can't believe it, Ted! She and her husband have a place on our lake, right near our house, and they are good friends of ours. I never dreamed we would come up with a connection that good. I think that'll be a great way to break the ice and get on friendly terms with Zander at the very beginning," said Luke with excitement.

"I'm pretty excited, too, Luke. What a great and helpful coincidence," Ted agreed. "If I can't take this deposition, and obviously I can't, I'm glad I have you to do it. I already feel a lot better."

The next day, a group of attorneys and parties convened at Alexander Carr's home. There were Ted and Rod, and Luke Green. There was a lawyer, Will Chambers, representing Mr. Carr's brokerage firm that had also been named as a defendant for allowing Ted, pursuant to the Probate Court Order, to administer Mr. Carr's Trust. There was another lawyer, Tay Messer, representing the interests of Mr. Carr's bank. There was Jason Smith, representing the Estate of the deceased John Carr. Of course, there was Mona Shadduck, who never acknowledged Ted's presence at the deposition. Ted was a friend of and had an excellent relationship with Will, who at one time had worked at Ted's Firm, and Ted had in fact worked closely with Will before Will joined another Firm. He knew Tay casually and had at one time done legal work for Tay's father. He also had a cordial and respectful relationship with Jason Smith, although he had not seen or talked with Jason since the day Ted had catalogued all the valuables at Mr. Carr's home shortly after John Carr's death. Jason was there primarily as an observer, and he said he did not intend to ask any questions unless some unexpected issue came up. At least it did not appear that any of the lawyers for third parties would be antagonistic toward Ted on account of any problematic past relationship, and perhaps they would take a positive view of Ted's position that could be helpful. Kate Carr Ross was there, and two of her brothers, Kim and Bruce, and their wives, were there as well.

The deposition was to be video recorded, as well as transcribed in written form, by a court reporter. The equipment for recording the deposition was all in place, but Mr. Carr was not yet present. However, the upstairs elevator whirred, and the group watched as Mr. Carr descended and stepped out of the elevator on the arms of Rand Carr and Jesse Carr. Ted Born made it a point to be near the elevator and to smile broadly at and greet Mr. Carr as he got out of the elevator, hoping Mr. Carr would know and remember Ted was there, notwithstanding his poor eyesight and memory lapses. Ted knew it was less likely Mr. Carr would say negative things about him if Mr. Carr knew Ted was present and, with his macular degeneration and the crowd of people there, it would have been possible that he could otherwise have gone through the entire deposition without knowing Ted was present.

Before the deposition started, Luke walked over to the chair where Mr. Carr was seated and extended his hand, which he took. "Mr. Carr, I am Luke Green, and I am so glad to meet you. I understand we have a mutual good friend, Sarah Knight. Aren't you her godfather?" "Yes, I am," replied Mr. Carr, "and she is a lovely young lady, one of my favorites." "Well, she is one of my favorites, too. She and her husband have a house on the same lake that we do, almost next door, and my wife and I see them a lot, and I think she's great. Now, I am glad I know her godfather." "And I'm glad to know you, Mr. Luke," Mr. Carr responded.

Then the deposition began. Luke started by saying, "Mr. Carr, we met just before the deposition and found out we had a mutual friend that we both thought highly of. Now I want to tell you that I am also a friend of Ted Born, who I think you also know and who is another friend of yours. Do you know Ted Born?"

"Oh, yes. He's been my lawyer and friend for I don't know how many years," he answered.

"I am a friend of Ted Born and I am here as a lawyer representing him, and I just want to ask you a few questions. You referred to Mr. Born as your lawyer. Do you regard him as your lawyer today?"

"Oh, yes."

"Has he ever done anything to you that would cause you to want to replace him as your lawyer?" Luke asked.

"Oh, no. He has always taken good care of me in whatever I've needed."

"Did you have a brother, John Carr, who passed away some time back?"

"Yes, he was my favorite, and my best friend. I've never known what happened," he said regretfully.

"And had you given him your power of attorney, and made him your Trustee, and named him to be the Executor of your estate?" Luke asked.

"I just don't remember anything about a Trust, but I know I had wanted him to help me take care of my business," he struggled to recall.

"And if your brother John died before you, or was unable to help you, did you name someone else to be a sort of backup or alternate to help you with your financial affairs or to handle your estate after your own death?" Luke asked.

"Yes, I think I did. Was it Mr. Born?" he asked.

"I think you are correct, Mr. Carr," observed Luke. "And did Mr. Born meet with you and discuss his taking over the responsibilities that your brother John had once had?" "I think he did," Zander answered.

At that point Luke Green noted that he understood Mr. Carr had difficulty reading because of his macular degeneration, but he made exhibits of the most recent power of attorney, Trust document and Will that named Born as his alternate, and they were offered in evidence without objection. He then said, "Mr. Carr, I want to state for the record that each of these three exhibits names Ted Born as your alternate and names no one else. Is that the way you recall it also?" He agreed.

"Now, Mr. Carr, did Mr. Born ever do anything or fail to do anything he was authorized to do under these documents that caused you to want to replace him with someone else?" He answered, "I don't think so."

"Do you believe Mr. Born would take good care of you and your interests?" Luke asked.

"Oh, yes, I'm sure he would," he answered.

"Do you still regard Mr. Born as a friend?" Luke asked. "Yes, very much so," he answered.

"Do you ever remember signing any documents to replace Mr. Born with anyone else?" He answered, "No."

"Did you ever authorize any attorney or attorneys to sue Mr. Born on your behalf?" Luke asked.

"Heavens, no. Why would I do that?" Mr. Carr seemed bewildered.

"Do you know anyone named Mona Shadduck, Mr. Carr?" Luke asked.

Mr. Carr thought for a moment and then said, "No. No. Now seems like I met someone with a name like that once. I don't remember."

Ted Born was sitting in a chair directly across the coffee table from where Mr. Carr was seated. He wasn't sure Mr. Carr could discern who he was with his vanishing eyesight, but Ted spoke to him before the deposition started to let him know where he, Ted, was sitting. But he need not have feared that Jesse and Mona would have successfully "prepped" him to say bad things about Born. Indeed, his testimony astonished everyone present with his support of Ted. If he had been coached or prepped to be negative toward Born, his poor short-term memory had blotted it out, and his long-term memory of a positive relationship came out strongly, better than Born had expected. Ted kept expecting Shadduck to interrupt or ask for a break, but, strangely, she did not. Ted was speculating in his mind that Shadduck was likely embarrassed to interrupt the deposition, that had just gotten started, for the obvious purpose of coaching the witness to change his testimony, given the fact that the video was recording everything, and her disruptive action would be interpreted in Court later as desperation and an admission that Mr. Carr was not competent on his own to give testimony favorable to Jesse. Indeed, in light of his testimony, Born wondered if, in Mr. Carr's frame of mind, he was coachable at all, so any interruption would be futile and perhaps counterproductive. Shadduck might also have been influenced by Luke Green's reputation as a recent past bar president and a premier trial lawyer, and she probably did not want to play games with him. In any case, Shadduck remained silent through the damaging testimony Mr. Carr was giving relative to her side of the case.

Luke kept asking him some of the same questions over and over, worded slightly differently, to protect against any argument that Mr. Carr had simply had a slip of the tongue and did not really mean what he had been saying. Then Luke decided to ask the witness some questions about Jesse, feeling that it would be better to have his comments about Jesse come out under his own questioning rather than under Mona's questioning. But it was risky to ask such a question without knowing in advance what the answer was likely to be, and he proceeded cautiously. "Mr. Carr," Luke asked, "you have a brother named Jesse, do you not?" He nodded affirmatively. "Have you always gotten along well with each other?"

"Well, he's my brother, we've mostly made up, but sometimes we didn't see things the same way. I can't remember any examples. He's been by to see me some lately," Mr. Carr said.

"Did you ever ask him to take the place of Mr. Born in looking after you and your finances?" Luke asked

"No, I didn't. He did say he wanted to help me, and I'm glad to have some help." Mr. Carr said.

"Did Jesse Carr ever ask you to sign any papers or documents he brought to you?"

"I don't think so. Every once in a while, I have to sign something, like income taxes or something. I don't remember anything Jesse brought me to sign." Mr. Carr said.

"Did Rand Carr ever bring you anything to sign?"

"I. don't remember anything recently," as he frowned slightly and rubbed his chin.

"What about Mona Shadduck, did she ever bring you anything to sign?"

"Mona Shadduck? I'm trying to think. Do I know her? Name sounds a little familiar, but I don't know anything about any papers anyone like that brought me to sign."

"Mr. Carr, did anyone else ever come to you and ask you to sign papers replacing Mr. Born in any capacity?" Luke asked.

"No, I wouldn't do that. Nobody would ask me to do that," the witness said.

"Do you feel Jesse would take care of you and your financial affairs well?" Luke Green asked.

"He said he wanted to help me." Mr. Carr replied.

"Did he ever tell you he could help you better if you would sign some papers he had prepared?"

He paused and seemed to be thinking, then answered, "No, I don't remember any papers."

"Have you been a subscriber to the *New York Time*?" Luke asked.

"Oh, yes, forever."

"Did you know that Jesse had canceled your subscription to the *New York Times*?"

"No, I would never let him do that!" he answered emphatically.

"He didn't ask you?"

"No, sir."

"In his deposition, Jesse said he canceled it because you could not afford it. Is that right, that you could not afford the *Times*?"

Mr. Carr: "Oh, I will always be able to afford the *New York Times*."

Luke continued: "Who is your accountant, Mr. Carr?"

"Joe Henaker. He's such a fine man, been my accountant forever," he answered.

Luke: "Did you know that Jesse fired Joe Henaker and told him to have no further contact with you?"

Mr. Carr: "I just don't know what to say. Joe's always been my accountant. Did you say Jesse fired him? I'll hire him back."

Luke: "Mr. Carr, I am afraid he did fire Joe Henaker, said 'new blood' was needed."

Mr. Carr: "Jesse, is that so?" Jesse spoke up and said, "We'll talk about that later, Zander."

Luke: "Did you know Jesse attempted to fire your lawyer, Ted Born?"

Mr. Carr: "Is that why I haven't seen much of Ted lately?"

Luke: "Jesse ordered Ted to stay off your premises."

Mr. Carr: "Why, I never!"

Luke: "Did you know that Jesse seriously considered mortgaging your house?"

Mr. Carr: "There's never been a mortgage on my house. Absolutely not! I wouldn't think of it."

Luke: "Mr. Carr, Jesse believes he has the power to mortgage your house whether you like it or not."

Mr. Carr: "I would never let him do that."

Luke went on to ask Mr. Carr some questions taken from some common mental assessment tests, such as taking the numeral 91 as a starting point and subtracting the numeral 9 from it, and then subtracting 9 from that result, continuing on. Mr. Carr was unable to perform that arithmetic, and he failed the other questions as well. Luke got him to reaffirm his confidence in Ted Born a few more times, for good measure, and then he turned the questioning over to the lawyer for Mr. Carr's brokerage firm, Will Chambers. If anything, the testimony reinforced Luke Green's efforts, and strongly affirmed the point that Miss Carr did not intend to authorize any displacement of Ted Born or the CPA Joe Henaker, and, at most, Jesse's role was just to help him in an incidental brotherly manner. Then Tay Messer asked a few questions. Ted was nervous about the questions Will and Tay might ask because he had been so pleased with the results of Luke's examination that he didn't want anything to happen that might provide an opportunity for backtracking. But, in fact, both of their lines of questioning seemed to make the deposition more and more favorable to Ted.

Then there was a normal break in the deposition before continuing with the questioning by Mona Shadduck. During the break, Ted congratulated Luke on a superb job of handling the questions. Ted wondered if Jesse, Rand, and Mona would try to get Mr. Carr to change his testimony. Neither Ted nor Luke could imagine how this could be done in a 15-minute break, especially considering the deponent's short memory span. And there would be the danger of unanticipated answers that would be especially devastating to Jesse's side, if given in response to questions asked by Jesse's own lawyer, purporting to represent Alexander Carr. Ted, Luke, and their team wondered how Shadduck would approach her interrogation.

When the break was over and Shadduck took her turn at questioning, she elected not to challenge Mr. Carr on the basics of his testimony. For one thing, Shadduck purported to be the lawyer for Mr. Carr, and it would be unseemly to be seen as trying to impeach her own client's testimony. In addition, it was possible, even probable, that Mr. Carr would provide answers that would not be helpful to Jesse's cause. Yet, she knew she had to ask him some questions to avoid the appearance of totally conceding his testimony. So, she contented herself with asking a few background questions, asking Mr. Carr if he recognized that Shadduck was a lawyer representing him and his brother Jesse, to which Mr. Carr answered simply, "All right." She tried to get Mr. Carr to say that he and Jesse had never been "estranged" from each other, but the best she got out of that was a statement that "Jesse is my brother, and we've had ups and downs, but he says he wants to help me now." Although Ted could not imagine how Shadduck could "rehabilitate" Mr. Carr's testimony to make it substantially more favorable to Jesse, he still expected extensive questions attempting to divert attention away from the damage done to Jesse in Luke Green's session, and in the sessions of Will Chambers and Tay Messer. But Shadduck concluded her questions in short order. At the end of the deposition, Ted went to Mr. Carr, clasped his hand and thanked him for his testimony and expressed the hope that they would be seeing each other again soon.

Ted and Rod went to Luke Green's office after the deposition to compare notes on where they thought the deposition left them. "I thought it was devastating to the other side, Luke. Great lawyering!" Ted said. "We now have a neuro-psychiatrist's finding that Mr. Carr lacked the mental capacity to sign papers purporting to oust me in favor of Jesse, and now we have Mr. Carr's testimony that he had no intention to oust me and doesn't remember signing any documents to do so. He didn't totally support the estrangement, but he did say he and Jesse had had their ups and downs, and he took issue with some of Jesse's recent actions. The Jesse contingent is going to have to either accept his testimony, which makes our case, or say he did not know what he was saying, which shows he has dementia, which also makes our case. Maybe this will mark a turning point in this nightmare of a case, even prompt a movement toward a settlement or resolution of some sort. But we owe you a great debt of gratitude for your fine professionalism, Luke."

"Ted, it's an honor to work on your behalf. I love you like a brother, and I know you have the highest possible standards as a lawyer. I am just so sorry that you, of all people, have had to endure the scurrilous accusations that have been hurled at you. They've been malicious. Maybe justice will come out of all this trauma. We can already see some light at the end of the tunnel," Luke remarked hopefully.

In the meantime, Mona Shadduck was meeting with Jesse and Rand Carr, along with other Carr siblings and spouses who had attended Zander's deposition. Zander himself was back in his sitting room upstairs. There was a mixture of disappointment and grimness hovering over the meeting. "Unfortunately, Luke Green did a masterful job," Rand said, "but I guess there was nothing we could do to prep Dad any better. His short-term memory seems gone, still remembers some things from the past, but those memories are mainly of good relations with Ted Born and Joe Henaker, and that's what came out. He doesn't remember the things that have happened recently, where we've been helping him. We tried to steer him in our direction, but it was apparently doomed to failure."

Kate Carr Ross, the youngest child and only daughter of Zander, spoke up. "This is really what I was afraid of when we got into this tangled jungle. I thought all along we should just accept the plan that Dad had laid out, with Uncle John's approval, and let Ted do his thing with the power of attorney and Trustee. We're spending a lot of money, that we could all be inheriting, and it doesn't seem to be getting us anywhere. I don't see how it's possible to win in view of Dad's deposition: He was all full of praise and support for Ted Born, and if we say he has short-turn memory problems, we've really just validated Born's argument that Dad did not have mental capacity to execute the documents putting Uncle Jesse in control. So, where does that leave us, Mona?"

"OK," Mona said, "I think in all this negativity, we are forgetting some things. First, I will say that I anticipated he might say the kinds of things he said, based on our prep sessions, and I realized there was nothing we could do to change that. If I had tried to get him to change his testimony, I would have had egg on my face – we would have all had egg on our faces, legally and psychologically.

That's because we can't badger our own client, our own witness, into changing his story. There's no way to come out a winner if you try to undermine the testimony of the person you are trying to represent. But, having said all that, does it mean we have just been dealt a fatal blow to our case? No! Let's keep things in perspective."

Jesse interjected, "Well, I hope you can give us a positive perspective. You've told us all along that 'it's in the bag,' that we're going to win. And I want to know how you see the percentages shifting after what happened today. If you can get some good news out of all this, I want to hear it, and I need to hear it." Some of the other family members were nodding in agreement.

"OK. First, you have to remind yourself that, if this case goes to trial, it is going to be in the Circuit Court, before Judge Tryon. I am confident that he believes it makes no sense for Ted Born to run the Zander Carr show for a high fee when there are perfectly capable family members who will do the job without charge. If he gets any chance to rule with us, he's going to do that, I think. So, what is our argument we present to Judge Tryon? The argument is that the relevant point in time for determining competency was the date Zander signed the key papers. There is absolutely no evidence that he was incompetent at that time. There have been a psychologist and a psychiatrist who have evaluated Zander's mental capacity later, after the papers were signed. The one who did it earliest and closest to the time the key documents were signed, our expert witness, found he was competent. Born's expert witness, the psychiatrist, examined him about ten months later and found he was not mentally competent *at that time.* But he could have crossed the competency line during that ten-month period. Same reasoning on the deposition. It's been more than a year now – he is now 94 years old, going on 95. If he's not competent today, it doesn't mean he was not competent when he signed the relevant documents. And we have a presumption in the law that he was competent to sign any documents unless there is proof of incompetency at that moment in time. We are aided by the fact that his last will revision overseen by Ted Born occurred when she was 91, so Born can't argue he was incompetent at that point, because it would have been improper for him to handle the execution of that will revision if Zander was incompetent then. So, you start with a timeline where there is no dispute as to his competency at age 91 and for the sake of argument, let's say he is incompetent at age 94, nearly 95. Where's the proof that he was incompetent at age 93 which is the critical point when he signed the key documents? There is not any proof of incompetency at that time, and the law presumes competency. Now, Judge Tryon is looking for a way to rule in our favor, in my opinion. And I think this is the way to do it - no proof of incompetency at the critical time. All he will need is an excuse to rule for us, and I think we can provide it the way I just mentioned. Sure, the deposition today did not help us, but it is far from a knockout blow. We've still got the upper hand, as long as we have Judge Tryon."

Bruce Carr interjected, "Of course, between us here today, I think he has been slipping for a long time. I doubt he was fully competent when he took the house away from me in that will he did when he was 91. Somehow, Dad got influenced to think it was 'fairer' to the rest of you to put the house in his residuary estate. But Dad was a person who kept his word, his promises, and he had promised me that house, and I don't think he would have reneged on his promise if he had been fully at himself. But that's all water over the dam. Mona, I'm no lawyer, but this sounds like a slender reed you are relying on, and it's going to be costly in terms of legal expenses, and I don't know that the chances of winning, or the benefits resulting from the win, are worth the expense and the emotional toll this is taking on all of us. Certainly, Born wins if he is competent today, because he was very clear Dad never had any intention of replacing him."

"I am here as a family adviser at the invitation of some of you, and I recognize that I don't have any official connection with this litigation," said Jason Smith. "I'm just here to observe and give you my impressions for what they are worth, as the lawyer for John Carr's estate. So, I have no axe to grind, just my judgment as a long-time lawyer and friend of the family. Obviously, this deposition marked a critical moment today, in this case. I'm not sure I have digested it all. I think it's something we all need to think about and talk about. I don't know about you, but I need to sleep on it. No offense to you, Mona, I gather you are still pretty confident, but it is a serious matter. We just need to do some thinking and talking. Meanwhile, I need to go right now, but I will be in touch." The group broke up shortly thereafter. The atmosphere was somber.

CHAPTER FOURTEEN

A VERY LONG-SHOT MOVE

Ted and Rod were mulling the status of the litigation. "You know," remarked Ted, "it's been a week since Mr. Carr's deposition, which I thought was pretty much a homerun for us, and I really thought we might get an overture from the other side to settle the case. I've been hoping they would reach out to us. I don't want to initiate settlement talks because I think Jesse and his crew would interpret it as a plea for peace at any price, and it would end up hurting settlement prospects instead of advancing them. I keep telling the Executive Committee that the Zander Carr deposition positions us to get a favorable settlement, and that has somewhat relieved the pressure from the Firm to dispose of the case. But the pressure isn't going to stay dormant for too long; it will come back.

We're having to fight this case internally as well as in the litigation forums on the outside, but that's life. We have to deal with it."

"Ted, can you think of any reason why they have not yet come to us for settlement?" asked Rod. "I would have thought they would come to us begging to settle."

"The only thing I can figure is the fact a trial date has been set and, if there is a trial, it will be before a Judge who seems hostile to our side. Even so, the hostility we perceived earlier might have been an initial impression, a shoot-from-the-hip sort of thing, and when Judge Tryon, or *any* Judge, for that matter, hears our evidence, I would think he would come out with a totally different view. But maybe our opposition knows something we don't know, or they think they do. Maybe we need to worry about Judge Tryon more than we think we should have to," Ted pondered.

"One thing we could do," offered Rod, "would be to file a summary judgment motion, saying we are entitled to judgment in our favor as a matter of law, based on the facts, without the need for a trial. That would smoke them out."

"That's a good possibility. But, to get summary judgment, you know, the facts must be undisputed. While we think the evidence is strongly in our favor, I am not at all sure the Judge would say they are entirely undisputed. Generally, mental capacity is one of those things that can't be mathematically ascertained with certainty, and I suspect the Judge will want to hear evidence, consider the demeanor of witnesses, and that sort of thing – all of which leaves room for argument, even if the evidence strongly favors us. You know, Judges also sometimes have a way of sitting on these motions for summary judgment, even holding them over for consideration after trial, which of course defeats their whole purpose. But they can do that, and Judge Tryon might. I'm not sure the summary judgment route will work in this case. Although I love summary judgment motions, and they have often been my bread and butter, I am afraid that if we file for one and don't get a favorable ruling early on, we'll be stuck with a trial we don't want, before a Judge who might well be hostile."

"Well," noted Rod, "if we don't get the summary judgment, it might mean subjecting Mr. Carr to the stress of trial, and there would be the publicity. One good thing is that the Philanthropist of the Year Award has already been quietly handed out to Mr. Carr, and there were minimal interviews of or statements by him in that connection, so we have dodged that bullet of being pilloried in the press for suing a philanthropic former client who is elderly and infirm. That helps us some with the Executive Committee too."

"Right," agreed Ted. "I do have one thought, Rod. I have been suppressing it because it is such a long shot, but maybe it is time to take some long shots. I am talking about asking the Supreme Court to issue a writ of mandamus ordering the Circuit Court to defer to the jurisdiction of the Probate Court. If we were successful, it would deprive Jesse and crew of their one ace-in-the-hole. Even if not successful, it would likely get the message to the Circuit Judge that he needs to be very fair."

"Wow! You are right that mandamus would be a long shot, a very long shot," said Rod. "The Supreme Court almost never grants them. They don't like to pre-judge how the trial courts handle their dockets, and they want to be sparing in granting those motions so as not to encourage their use and inundate the Supreme Court with more mandamus motions."

"You are correct on all counts, Rod," observed Ted. "But I have some glimmer of hope we might be successful in this instance, for several reasons. First, the case was filed in the Probate Court first, and the other side has really engaged in forum-shopping in filing an unnecessary parallel case in the Circuit Court. The Supreme Court does not like forum-shopping. The second reason is that Mona Shadduck has made such outrageous and intemperate accusations against me that I think it might offend the Supreme Court and get its attention. Third, one of the members of the Supreme Court is a former Probate Judge and will possibly understand that this trial, if there is to be one, is more appropriate to the Probate Court where the Probate Judge has dealt with so many similar types of cases, more so by far than the Circuit

Court Judges. Finally, we have a young lawyer, Matt Ariton, who has been clerking in the Supreme Court and knows how to prepare mandamus motions to maximize their impact. Let's get his help. I think it is worth the try. In this case, I would give our probability at about 20%, instead of the usual 1%."

The mandamus petition was prepared and filed with the state Supreme Court. In short order, Born and Olson got an opposition brief from Shadduck, predictably making over-the-top accusations of unethical conduct and greedy motivations on the part of Born, notwithstanding Alexander Carr's glowingly positive comments about Born. If it served no other purpose, Shadduck's hot-tempered response gave notice that she and her parties had no interest in settlement, even though objectively the evidence had not moved in a direction favorable to her positions. In the meantime, the parties continued their discovery. Rand Carr's deposition was taken, and he claimed he could not remember if he had been present when the document was signed to change the power of attorney holder from Ted to Jesse, although he acknowledged making the arrangements for the original lawyer, Greg Tween, to draft it, at Jesse's request, as he told it. He admitted he might have been present when his Dad signed the replacement Trust and the replacement Will. He testified that admittedly his Dad did not read, and could not read, any of the documents because of his poor eyesight, and no one attempted to read the lengthy documents to him word-for-word. He said Mr. Carr was told these were updates, and he thought his Dad understood that Born was being replaced, but he could not remember just what was said. He admitted being present at his Dad's deposition and heard his statements that he did not remember signing or intending to sign any documents replacing Ted Born. He could not explain the discrepancies in his recollection versus his and Jesse's recollections.

Rand's deposition and other discovery had to be completed in order to get ready for the scheduled trial in the Circuit Court. Shortly afterward, as the parties were preparing for trial in the Circuit Court, a computer printer in Ted's office began rumbling, and it appeared to be spewing out a copy of an order issued by the Supreme Court. Ted braced himself for the worst, as each of the several pages came off the printer. He could not believe his eyes when he read the unanimous Supreme Court decision, *granting* the Writ of Mandamus and ordering the Circuit Court to stay all proceedings in this matter, pending disposition of the corresponding litigation in the Probate Court! Ted grasped the order and pressed it against his chest. Then he planted a kiss on it and hastened to Rod's office with the good news. "Rod!" he said, "Jesse just lost his trump card! The Supreme Court granted our mandamus petition! Can you believe it? Actually, they *should* have granted it and they were right to grant it, but they grant so few, I had braced myself for disappointment. The odds were so far against us, but we won! We don't have to go to trial immediately, and if we ever do, it will be in the Probate Court where the

Judge understands how family members sometimes 'lead' elderly relatives and get them to do things they never would have done in years when their mental faculties were normal. Do you think Mona will want to talk to us about settlement now?"

Rod, too, was overjoyed. "I just can't believe it," he said. "Things looked so bleak for a while, and then they began to improve as we got into discovery and the truth began to come out. Even so, I never would have dreamed the Supreme Court would preempt the Circuit Court in favor of the Probate Court. If Jesse and Mona have got any sense, they will want to come to us on bended knee, begging to settle."

Then Ted raised a highly pertinent question: "Rod, on what basis could we settle with them now, assuming they would want to settle? After we have found out about Jesse's scheming and outright dishonesty, could we allow him to participate cooperatively with us in the managing of Mr. Carr's financial affairs? Maybe we could have done that at one point on the basis that it was the best we could get, and at least was better than nothing, but now - we now hold the winning hand, and if we let him be a part of managing her financial affairs, wouldn't we be doing exactly what we vowed to Mr. Carr we would never let happen?"

"Maybe we could let him manage the household staff, or something like that, keeping him out of the financial things," proposed Rod. "Let's tell the Executive Committee about this. They've never cared much about winning, really didn't think it was possible. They just wanted to get out. Presumably, this pretty much puts an end to the liability of you, Ted, and of the Firm, and they should be happy about that. And the malpractice insurer ought to be happy as well. But they have attached such a negative attitude to the whole case that I suspect their emphasis is still going to focus on extricating us from the litigation, not winning it."

Although a lot of Firm lawyers congratulated Ted and Rod, nobody from the Executive Committee came to do so, although they did seem to understand that the case had moved into a posture where it was no longer a serious potential liability. Ted thought it strange that the Executive Committee's emphasis had been on "getting out," instead of winning, and why winning did not seem to make them particularly happy, especially when viewed as a vindication of a client. Nevertheless, everybody, including the Executive Committee, was willing to give Jesse and his side time to capitulate, which they hoped would happen sooner rather than later.

CHAPTER FIFTEEN

A CRACK IN THE WALL

The telephone rang in Ted Born's office. "Hello,
Ted. This is Jason Smith. You know I don't have
any official role in this litigation over who's going to have
Zander Carr's power of attorney or the trusteeship of his
Trust. I am in some way on the outside looking in. But
I am representing the estate of John Carr, and Zander's
children all look to me as their adviser on family matters,
mostly legal, but some just practical judgment calls. You
might have thought the family was united behind Jesse,
but that's really not so. There have been doubts from the
beginning, but they kept being assured by Mona that Jesse
would win as a foregone conclusion, and most of them just
kind of lay back passively and went along with it."

"Hi, Jason. Thanks for calling. I have been hoping that was the case, but of course I could not ethically speak directly to any of them since they were represented by Mona in the litigation, and any conversation would have to go through her – an exercise in futility. So, we've had to just handle things in a formal way through depositions and pleadings in the litigation," Ted responded.

"Well, you handled everything properly, of course. But the Carr heirs felt boxed in also because they really wanted to talk with you and ask questions and get your perspective, and they likewise had to hang back. But some of them, I think most of them, are having very serious reservations about the way things have been handled by Jesse. He seems to be asserting his authority, and he is a stubborn guy. Even Rand might be edging away from him. As I said, Mona has been telling them that Jesse is a sure winner, that everything is going perfectly," Smith continued.

"She 'thoughtfully' got the word to me also, by an indirect conduit, to the effect that she had it all sewed up and that I was going to face financial ruin as well as destruction of my reputation – she sent that message via Greg Tween, indirectly, to my partner Rod Olson," Ted commented. "It was a low point for me, but I thought long and hard about it, and decided to put it all on the line," Ted soberly reflected, remembering the personal trauma he experienced at a point in the case when things were not going well for him.

"And I admire you for it, Ted. But, anyway, Zander's deposition was a real wakeup call for the group. For the first time, they saw Zander and heard Zander as he affirmed his desire for you to be in charge. Even if you discount some of what he said because of dementia, still it came out loud and clear that you were the right alternate for him and that, if he signed any contrary papers Jesse stuck in front of him, he did not appreciate what he was signing. As a result of that deposition, most of them understood that Zander wanted you to be 'it' and also that you were probably going to win. Mona lost all credibility with most of the family after that deposition, when they sat there and saw the real Zander come out. After all, he is their father, always admired by them, even if these are not his best days. In any case, the family all gathered afterward to hear what Mona had to say, and Mona made the point that, even if Zander was not competent today, there was no evidence he was incompetent months ago when he signed Jesse's papers, and the law would presume him to be competent at that time, in the absence of contrary evidence. This was reported to me, as I had already left right after Zander's deposition was over. Seemed to me it was incredibly unrealistic to use that line of thinking to support Jesse's side of the lawsuit, because Zander's incompetence now would certainly be circumstantial evidence of incompetence a matter of months earlier, plus his eyesight problems and other health issues would combine to indicate vulnerability and undue influence. To me, it was clear that Jesse took advantage of

Zander's overall condition, mental and physical, to get him to sign paperwork favorable to Jesse and adverse to you, that Zander would not have signed under normal circumstances - undue influence, if nothing else.

"In any case, the Carr heirs left the deposition shaken and not sure what to do or think. They tended to lean in your direction, Ted, but one problem is that they really don't know you," Smith related.

Born interjected, "Of course, I knew that was a problem I had. In the very beginning, in the first few days of my service as Mr. Carr's alternate, I had asked Rand Carr to arrange for a meeting between me and all the heirs. He kept putting me off, and the meeting never took place, and now I know why – any such a meeting might have weakened or destroyed Jesse's effort to consolidate family support for him. Then, after the new paperwork came out and we got into litigation, I could not have such a meeting. I was cut off from the heirs, as well as from Mr. Carr."

"What I am here to tell you, Ted, is that I think there is a way to have such a meeting. I suggest you meet with the women, the wives of Zander Carr's sons – except Rand's wife Tammy, of course – and Kate would like to meet with you also. I think she has already advised Mona that she is exiting or has already exited the wall of Carr support for Jesse. She has been heavily influenced from the beginning by the belief that, if her father worked with you and approved your being the alternate, then she should honor her father's judgment in the absence of some good reason to reject it. Her Dad's deposition pretty much sealed it for Kate. As for the others, they were strongly affected by that deposition, but had not quite come to the point of openly opposing their uncle. But then the Supreme Court's mandamus order came out, and it cut the heart out of whatever logical basis there was for thinking Jesse might win. I feel pretty sure the Probate Judge is going to see this as family members taking advantage of an elderly relative's infirmities to favor themselves against the true wishes of their own father. So, in their minds, the case has turned around 180 degrees, and most of them are not unhappy with that, because they've never really trusted or respected Jesse anyway. And back to my original point, the women can meet with you, because Mona does not represent them and has never represented them, and Kate has specifically withdrawn. The idea is, that the wives will go back to their husbands and report on the meeting with you, and the husbands – who already lean toward you and who are on the cusp of defecting – they will come around completely if they feel they could be comfortable working with you. Can we set up such a meeting, Ted?" Smith asked.

"Of course," Ted said, "I would welcome it. In addition to the reasons you gave for justifying the meeting, bear in mind also that I am currently functioning as Trustee under the original Probate Court order, and they have a legitimate reason to meet with me on account of my management of the Trust. It is clear to me that Jesse has followed a policy of isolating Mr. Carr from everything and everybody who might raise questions about his takeover - a scorched earth policy. He forbade me to come onto Mr. Carr's home premises. He's done the same thing with Joe Henaker, Mr. Carr's long-time CPA, told him never to set foot on her property. And Jesse didn't want any family members to have any contact with me. It has been a deliberate 'isolate and control' strategy. They - through you, their counsel and adviser - have approached me to set up a meeting. I don't see why we can't ethically do it. Bring them on!"

CHAPTER SIXTEEN

THE MEETING

On the appointed day, a group of ladies, accompanied by Jason Smith, arrived in the reception room of Born's Firm. Ted went out to greet them and was introduced one-by-one to them. They had seen Ted at Zander's deposition, but had largely stayed to themselves on the sidelines, and Ted had been busy conversing quietly with Luke Green and with focusing his attention on the deposition. So, this was really the first introduction. There was Kate Carr Ross, the only daughter of Mr. Carr, and there was Amanda, wife of Bruce Carr, and Jennifer, wife of Kim. Ted asked them to follow him into one of the Firm's larger conference rooms, noted for the marble conference room table with multi-colored stone inlay. It was early morning, and Ted had arranged for doughnuts and muffins, along with the usual coffee and tea offerings.

"I'm really glad to meet all of you. Thanks for coming. I had tried to have just such a meeting with you and all the Carr family members right after John's passing - asked Rand to arrange it, in fact - but it never got done, and we found ourselves in this unfortunate litigation. It could possibly have all been avoided if we had had that meeting. So, I'm glad to have the meeting now, even if the circumstances are a little different," Ted said at the outset.

Jason Smith took advantage of a slight pause and said, "Ted, why don't you tell them something about yourself. They really want to know more about you. We can talk about the case later, but I think you should start by telling them something about yourself, your background and experience and whatever you want to tell them."

"There isn't much to tell, actually. I am just an ordinary person, happen to be a lawyer, trying to be ethical and trying to serve the interests of my clients, trying to be faithful to them. I've had some tough times in my life, some gratifying times too. Somehow, I end up getting cases that are real bears, but I've learned that when the challenges come, I have to just keep on swinging. God must enjoy seeing me swing, because he keeps sending me tough cases, like this one, but maybe this is the toughest of all, because I was not only defending a client but also was defending myself. I am approaching the end of my professional career, a good, clean career, and I stand accused of resisting my client's wishes for my own financial benefit. It hurts. I don't live that way. I'm just an ordinary person, but not someone who would ever betray a client, regardless the cost to me, financially, emotionally or otherwise," Ted responded.

"How did you decide that the right thing to do was to fight Jesse? You must have wanted to control Zander's affairs a lot to take on that fight. Why?" asked Kate.

"No, no, I did not want to control your Dad's affairs at all," said Ted. "I would much rather just continue being the same old lawyer I have always been. I took it on because I made a vow, in fact several times I made a vow, to Mr. Carr, that I would never let Jesse have anything to do with his financial matters. He insisted and made me promise that many times. I thought it was a hypothetical, a moot question. Mr. Carr was still in good health at the time and so was John Carr, and I never thought the issue would ever come up. But Mr. Carr extracted a solemn commitment from me, and I literally told him that I 'vowed' I would never let that happen. It was maybe one of the more foolish things I have ever done because, if I had thought it through, I would have realized that there was no way I could guarantee that Jesse would be kept away from Mr. Carr's financial affairs - I did not have complete control over that. The Probate Court or the Circuit Court could have something to say about that. As it turned out, the sadly ironic thing was that I was trying to live up to my vow to one Mr. Carr, while resisting the actions of another Mr. Carr who signed documents putting Jesse in charge. Should I carry out the repeated instructions from the Mr. Carr whom I had known and represented for a quarter of a century, or should I honor the actions of a new and different Mr. Carr who is saying just the opposite through new papers he signed? I never wanted the position of alternate, agreed to it at his request as an accommodation, and I would have gladly relinquished all claims to be the 'in charge' designee.

"Why didn't I? Because the Mr. Carr I knew would never have displaced me without doing me the courtesy of telling me politely that he had had a change of mind. He wouldn't have done it that way. In addition, I had personally observed some slippage in his mental capacity, and even John Carr told me he was concerned about that. I had been with Mr. Carr just a day or two before Jesse flung the new power of attorney at me; I was trying to help Rand, actually. At that time, he said nothing to me about any intention to replace me, and it would have been a perfect and natural time and place to do so, if he had been contemplating such a move. So, I had to decide which Mr. Carr was the one whose instructions I should follow, and I felt I should honor, and was morally required to honor, the commitment I had made to the Mr. Carr of a 25-year professional relationship, at least to the extent of asking the oversight of the Probate Court. The only way I could keep Jesse from getting control was to be prepared to assume these responsibilities myself, if approved through the judicial process. So, I never wanted to manage his financial affairs, but it was the only way to keep Jesse from taking over."

"Did you consider that your efforts could tarnish Zander's reputation by branding him as an incompetent at the end of a storied career?" asked Jennifer Carr.

"Yes, I thought about that at length and struggled with it, over and over. I tried to handle the problem without alleging mental incapacity that could be embarrassing to his legacy. I just asked the Probate Court to give me instructions as to what to do, whether to honor the new power of attorney or not. I thought the matter could be quietly resolved in a hearing after, maybe, 30 or 40 days, and then it would be all over. But Jesse escalated the process, and, through Mona, he made me a targeted defendant, accusing me of unethical conduct, fraud, self-dealing, and trying to destroy a fine man's reputation just to get a fee. I had no choice but to contest these outrageous allegations, which Mona filed in court for all the world to see. It was MY reputation that got sullied, much more so than Mr. Carr's. An allegation of fraud and dishonesty is a lot worse than an allegation of dementia, which at worse evokes sympathy. Any judicial vindication of my position probably will not entirely catch up with and mend the damage that has already been done to my reputation. But the responsibility of a lawyer is to put his client's interests first, not his own. And knowing that

Mr. Carr was a fighter who would never allow anyone to take advantage of him, I felt he would want his plans and intentions carried out, even at the risk of dementia coming to the fore.   So, I stuck with the case, and it seems to be turning in the right direction now – which is to say, in favor of the Mr. Carr I have known for so long."

"What about the fees you planned to charge for your power of attorney work and Trustee work? Were. you really planning to charge $900,000? In fact, Mona's latest figure is $1.8 million? What were you going to charge?" asked Kate. "Because your fees seem to have been a catalyst that set off the campaign to get you removed. What's the story there?"

"That is just plain baloney! I have always charged Mr. Carr my regular hourly rates - not a fee based on the size of his estate. And I had tried to structure my handling of the power of attorney work so that there would be in place a system for dealing with normal issues, paying bills, getting groceries, transporting him places, and that kind of thing, to minimize my personal time and involvement, while still taking care of Mr. Carr's needs. He was living a fairly simple life, no travel, mainly spending the day in his sitting room. I would have had to be involved only minimally. Of course, I intended to make some purely social visits to Mr. Carr, but I certainly would not have charged for those. I would estimate that $25,000 to $30,000 a year might have covered it, including both the Trustee fees *and* our legal fees - nothing even close to the crazy figures that somehow got circulated. Remember that there would always have been legal fees for purely legal work, regardless of who the Trustee was. Whether spreading this misinformation was deliberate or based on a very sincere mistaken belief, I can't say. But I could have cleared this up if I had known it was an issue and if we had had the family meeting I wanted," Ted responded.

Jason Smith spoke up: "I am embarrassed to say I might have inadvertently been a cause of your fee being an issue. Rand asked me what you *could* charge, and based on the size of Zander's estate, I told him the *maximum* would be around $900,000, but the Court would have to review and approve it. I guess I should have emphasized the word 'maximum.' Some lawyers might try to bill a big number like that, but you don't operate that way, I'm sure. I feel very sorry if I caused this to be an issue."

"Jason, I doubt you caused this. Certainly, Greg Tween or Mona Shadduck could have clarified it. I would have been glad to clarify it I had been able to have that meeting that never took place. The fee rumor was just a talking point to justify the takeover. It's just that simple," Ted said.

Jason spoke up again. "Ted, you were overly modest, in the extreme, to call yourself 'an ordinary person.' You've headed numerous civic organizations, and have served as a trustee of several charities, and you have won some phenomenal lawsuits. You are on everybody's peer-reviewed list of premier lawyers, in multiple fields. Tell them a little more about all your accolades."

Ted smiled sheepishly and replied, "Accolades? I have learned something about accolades. They are really the 'thank-you notes' the community or others give you for something you've done that they appreciate. It might be represented by a paper certificate or a plaque or just inclusion on some list somewhere. They are just polite ways of saying 'thank you.' You are fooling yourself if you think they really mean more than that. Next year few people will remember that you got some honor, and the year after that almost nobody will know or remember. The value of accolades is just to let you know someone appreciates something you've done, and after you feel good about that for a very short while, the 'accolades' really mean nothing. Save them and show it to the grand-children if you like, but it means nothing more. How many people can tell you who won the Nobel prizes last year? Not many. And they're the biggies. No, Jason, I no longer try to assign any value beyond momentary satisfaction when someone or some group recognizes me, or any other person. It might look good in an obituary to show a list of awards or recognitions accumulated by some newly departed soul over a lifetime, and a random reader might say, 'that's nice,' and toss the paper into the recycling bin, without another thought. But I know I am just an ordinary person who somehow has been exposed to and been a small part of some extraordinary experi-ences. Those experiences have been a part of my learning process, and that is where the value lies, not in what some might call 'accolades.' You learn that, to most people, the only question that matters is, 'what can you do for me now?' If any of you will work with me and believe in me, that is appreciated. But all you get is an ordinary person, an ordinary person who tries - yeah, tries hard."

They all shook his hand, seemed upbeat, and went their ways.

CHAPTER SEVENTEEN

THE WAIT

Kate Carr Ross made a visit to her Dad with a mission in mind. "Dad, how are you feeling?"

"Not good. I don't know what's the matter, Kate. I just don't feel good," Alexander Carr answered.

"Do you feel worried, do you feel tense, and do you sleep well?" asked Kate.

"I just feel mixed up, kind of lost, and, no, I don't sleep well." Zander answered with a distant, blank look on his face.

"Are you worried about the litigation?" Kate inquired.

"What litigation?" Zander asked.

"Do you remember that there is some litigation between Uncle Jesse and Ted Born about who's going to
help you manage your affairs?" Kate asked.

Zander frowned and hesitated. "I don't know. Seems
like I've heard something about a lawsuit, but I don't
remember. Now, tell me what it's about. Will it have any
effect on me?"

"Yes, Daddy. It could affect you. Your brother
Jesse got you to sign some papers to put him in charge of
your affairs, your money, your house, really your life, and
there's a lawsuit about that. In fact, the lawyers took your
deposition in that lawsuit, and the outcome could affect
you." Kate replied.

"I just don't know. I've had a good life. I don't like to
worry about things like that," Zander said with his head
slightly bowed.

"You can stop this lawsuit, Daddy. Only you can put
an end to it right now. Jesse is losing, and he is running
up the expenses and has the whole family tied up in knots.
Will you tell Uncle Jesse to drop it?" Kate was pleading.

"I'll see. Jesse says he just wants to help me, and
sometimes I need help. I need someone besides my sitters
that I can talk with. Jesse comes to see me sometimes,"
Zander replied vaguely.

"I do think you need to stop this litigation that is tearing up the family and wasting your money. Please try to tell Uncle Jesse to drop it," Kate reinforced her request.

"Kate, I don't understand these things. You will see when you get my age. I just want to feel better and be happier. I don't feel good and I'm not happy. I've had a good life. I'm tired. Thanks for coming by to see me," Zander said.

Kate left her father's house and went by to see her brother Bruce. "Bruce, I have just come from Daddy's house, and I had a talk with him and urged him to tell Uncle Jesse to drop this lawsuit. It's not doing any good. It is costing a lot of money, and it's wrong. It's not just that Daddy wanted Ted Born to manage things. Uncle John agreed with that as well, and everything would have gone much better if it had just been left that way. As it is, it seems to me we've had all this turmoil for nothing. After sitting through Daddy's deposition, which was so favorable to Born, I don't see how Jesse can expect to win, but, even in the face of that, nothing's happening. Oh, yes, one other thing happened. The Supreme Court shut down the Circuit Court litigation which was the big hope for Jesse's case. Tell me, why is this litigation still going on?"

"Kate, I think it is still going on because Jesse is determined and convinced that he has a divine right to manage Dad's affairs," Bruce replied. "That lawyer of his - what's her name, Ramona or something? Anyway, she keeps feeding him assurances that she still has the case under control, and that she will win it. Well, that's what Uncle Jesse wants to hear, wants to believe, and he's not a lawyer and can't evaluate it. If it comes from the mouth of a lawyer that's on his side, then that settles the matter as far as he's concerned. He is possessed and consumed by the prospect of seeing this case to the bitter end, even if it really *will* be bitter for him. But in his mind, he still thinks he will win. Anyone who tells him anything different is a traitor to the family in his mind."

"The lawyer's name is 'Mona,' I think," Kate volunteered. "I understand she keeps saying there's still a good chance to win, even though we are now back in the Probate Court. She is still saying there's no proof Daddy was mentally incapacitated at the time he signed the papers that made him 'it,' and there's a presumption he was competent. Then Mona says she can appeal if there is a loss. She puts a lot of emphasis on the fact that Uncle Jesse is Daddy's brother, his only living brother or sister, and it is so 'natural' for him to be the one in charge, thinks that argument could carry the day, even in the face of Daddy's deposition. But it's not going to happen. We are burning money over Uncle Jesse's stubbornness. And he's making Ted Born spend money to contest it."

"What kind of luck did you have in your meeting with Dad?" Bruce inquired. "He has a soft spot for you, Kate. If anyone can get him to intervene, you're the one."

"I doubt I got anywhere. He doesn't even remember there is any litigation, just doesn't want to deal with it. Even if he had said he would tell Uncle Jesse to drop the lawsuit, I doubt he would remember it or follow through. His short-term memory is really shot. I don't know what else we can do. There is a war going on over him and his wealth, and he is oblivious to it. It's unbelievable! Dad was always so 'in control,' a person who planned and was so intimately involved in every detail. And now, the war and its battles are over for him, no more combat. It is amazing what age does to you. Well, I'm going to talk with Jason Smith and see if he can get the ear of Ted Born and maybe get him to initiate settlement talks, but I am not optimistic. Born now is holding the high cards and is not going to want to appear weak." Kate mused.

At about the same time, Rand Carr was talking with his Uncle Jesse at Jesse's home, notwithstanding the irritation of Jesse's wife Candace that Rand would come over when, she said, Jesse was not feeling well. "Are you not feeling well, Uncle Jesse?"

"Not so good, Rand. I feel tired, and I'm having some problems with my urinary track. Going to see the Doctor tomorrow, who'll probably give me a pill or something. What brings you here?" Jesse responded.

"Just wanted to talk about where we are in this lawsuit. I'm worried," said Rand.

"You don't need to worry, Rand. We're going to win. It's just going to take a little longer, that's all." Jesse advised.

"Is that what Mona is saying? I like Mona, and I recommended her to you, but things have not been going your way lately, and I don't see a favorable outcome for you. For one thing, the family is split. In the beginning all of us Carrs were together, with one unified voice – which was important. Now, Kate is openly opposed to our effort and at least a couple of the others are leaning against us. And then, we've got Daddy's deposition, which couldn't have gone much worse for you, and, after that, the Supreme Court said we have to go to trial in the Probate Court, which is probably not good - maybe not hopeless, but not good either. So, if we have to go to trial without a united front in the family, we could be in trouble. Do you think we should talk with the other side about settlement?" Rand asked.

"Hell, no! And damn NO!" said Jesse, with red-face anger and irritation at the very thought of settlement. "There's no way to settle this thing. Either I win or Born wins! I could never work with Born, and I doubt he would work with me, and, besides, I don't want him looking over my shoulder. Remember, we're right, and he's wrong. He's wrong! I'm your Dad's brother of 86 years. I'm the one who's known him the longest. Yeah, I do want to get my hands on the money, but I would take care of him, too. I would see that he was comfortable, might have to move him into a nursing home and sell the house, but he'd be taken care of. It might be a hard fight, but – WE ARE GOING TO WIN! It's common sense that his brother should be in charge, not some lawyer with dollar marks in his eyes. No compromise, and no talking about settlement! I think that lawyer will be so worried about his reputation, he'll beg to get out. It will take some time, but we have to be firm."

"Well, remember that you are his brother, but I am his son. I want money conserved, and I want Dad taken care of. Uncle Jesse, you know you can always talk things out with me, come what may. The good thing is, we don't have to decide that today. We can all think about it and take it one day at a time. Think it over. Hope you feel better and get a good report from the doctor. Of course, Mona has got to be paid, and our funds are getting kind of thin, as Born's controlling the Trust accounts where most of the money is. Guess I'd better be going. Again, take it easy, and good luck with the doctor visit."

Meanwhile, back at Born's law firm, the Executive Committee continued to be interested in when Born was going to settle the case. The Firm Administrator, acting as a messenger of the Executive Committee, dropped in and inquired, "How's the settlement option going, Ted?"

"At this point, there is no 'settlement option.' You can't rush these things. We've got about six months be- fore we have to go to trial in the case, and you know how lawyers are. They mostly settle on the courthouse steps, when they know that they otherwise will have to face the music in a real trial. We are well positioned legally, with the great results from Mr. Carr's deposition, and we think we are set for trial in a Court that will give us a fair shake, all you can ask for. Besides that, some of the Carr family members have seen the handwriting on the wall, and they've come over to our side, although most are being a bit quiet about it because they don't want to incur the wrath of their uncle. I don't think we have to worry as much any more about alienating the members of the influential Carr family, because they sat through Mr. Carr's deposition, and I have met with them and talked with Jason Smith, who advises them. They are coming over to our side if they are not already here with us. Of course, no one can guarantee anything, but I have been in a lot of cases, and I know something about settlement negotiation strategy. I feel like Jesse will come around and want to settle when the time comes. On the other hand, if I approach him or his lawyer right now about settlement, they will take it as a sign of weakness, making it impossible to settle or certainly hurting the prospects of a reasonable settlement. Remember, the case is shaping up well for settlement. If it takes a little while to get it done, that's okay, let's be patient. Most of the discovery has been done, and the case will be largely dormant for a while, so I see no downside for being patient," Born explained.

"Sounds logical to me. I will urge patience, but I think the consensus still is strongly in favor of settlement.

If you try the case and happen to win it, that would be good, in a way, but it would also leave some complications, because our malpractice carrier would still have problems with your serving in fiduciary capacities for Mr. Carr while the Firm also represents him, raising conflict of interest problems. And, if you lose, the Circuit Court case, though stayed at this moment, could then be reactivated and you would be exposed to all kinds of personal liability – as well as the Firm."

"I understand all that, but we can cross that bridge a little later," said Born. "We have to remember that our commitment for me to serve as a fiduciary was made years ago before there was any suggestion of a conflicts problem. I should be grandfathered in. But it's all a moot question at this point."

The Administrator commented that Born had had an outstanding career, and the Firm's concern was partly that, for Born's sake, it did not want anything to tarnish that reputation. Born expressed appreciation for the comments and interest in his reputation, but to himself he wished he could just be left alone to handle this, with the judgment he had shown in so many other cases.

A few weeks later, Ted got a call from Jason Smith, who said, "Hi, Ted. Just touching base with you. I think all the Carr family members favor your side in the litigation except maybe Rand, and we think he is really wanting to come around but feels obligated not to abandon his Uncle Jesse. But, of course, the family members are all largely being discreet about it right now. They don't want to unnecessarily irritate Jesse, or his wife Candace, both of whom have quite a temper. Are you having any discussions with Mona about settlement?"

"I appreciate the support of the family members, even if they are not advertising their feelings at this point. I hope they will come out at the trial, though, if we have to go to trial. All's quiet on the settlement front – total silence from Mona, and I hear she is egging Jesse on rather than advising him to settle. I don't understand why no move has been made, but there is still time to settle before trial."

CHAPTER EIGHTEEN

THE TRIAL

The trial date set by the Probate Court was approaching, with no sign that the Jesse Carr side was interested in any settlement. As had happened many times, Ted and Rod met in a conference room to review the status of the case. "Why do you think that is, Rod? Why would they not want to settle?" Ted asked rhetorically, knowing Rod had no answer.

"As we have mentioned before, it could be the old courthouse-steps play, that you get a better settlement when you are standing there on the courthouse steps, knowing you've got to go through trial and you don't want to - risk is too high, not well enough prepared, or you're tired and need a break from trials. Or - it could be that, with Jesse calling the shots, he's just too damned stubborn to make a realistic assessment and has convinced himself he's going to win. Or - maybe they know something we don't know, an ace up their sleeve. I don't know. Why do you think the other side did not use the 'Philanthropist of the Year' gala to finger us as an enemy of the wonderful, philanthropic Mr. Carr?" Rod asked in return.

"My best guess," said Ted, "is that Jesse had no idea what Mr. Carr would say if the press began asking questions about that, and he did not want to take a chance. No one can control what he might say at this point. Also, it would have introduced a sour note into the gala that would have been a real downer. After the way his deposition went, Jesse did not want to take a chance. As for Jesse's state of mind, I'm not sure he realizes how much support he has lost of the Carr family members. Except for Rand, they've all come over to our side now, or at least we think they have, and that puts Jesse and Rand out there by themselves - and Rand himself might even come over if he sees a loss is inevitable. Of course, while we think things are going well for us at this point, litigation is a strange thing. It's hard to make the evidence come out just the way you want it or expect it. We think Mr. Carr's deposition went well for us, but what if he shows up and recants everything he said in his deposition? You know, Rod, I always say that there's about a 25% chance of losing a case that should be strongly in your favor, and about a 25% chance of winning a case that is heavily weighted against you, and the other 50% of cases are tossups. Never forget that we could still lose this case.

The other side knows this, too. That's why we have to do everything possible to leave no stone unturned in our trial preparations."

"You say 'we,' but actually the lawyers on our side who'll be asking the questions will be from Luke Green's firm. We'll be sitting at the counsel table – or you will, I'll probably be out in the audience – because we can't represent ourselves. I know we will do a lot of the backstage planning, but it's tough sitting at the counsel table and not being able to participate actively, asking questions, making objections, addressing the Judge, and so on. Are you comfortable being the client when you are used to being the lead lawyer in the middle of a heated trial?" Rod probed.

"I've thought about that, Rod, and I'm resigned to my more 'subdued' role in this trial," Ted noted thoughtfully. "There are some good things about it. The Judge knows the Luke Green lawyers better than he knows me, because they practice in the Probate Court a lot more than I do. Also, the Probate Court is a bit more flexible about letting in evidence than the Circuit Court would be. Since this will be a non-jury trial, I would guess that, in a critical situation, the Judge might even allow me to get up and interject something. A lot of the case is going to be presented by depositions, and we know what's in those – and there's no risk of that changing. We will get to put our evidence on first, because we initiated things by filing the motion for instructions, and that puts us in the position of plaintiffs, with the right to go first. We'll put in our evidence, and we will call Jesse to the stand as an adverse and hostile witness as a part of our case, because I want the Judge to get his impression of Jesse through the questions we ask him, not the softball questions Mona might ask him. We'll probably do the same with Rand. When we get through with our case, I don't know who Mona might call as her witnesses. She will probably call her psychologist, although he seems lukewarm, hesitant to go too far out on a limb in view of all that has happened in this case since he made his original affidavit. She might call the guy from the St. Bartholomew Foundation who solicited the million-dollar gift, but he really doesn't know Mr. Carr, and he certainly is not qualified to be an expert on his mental capacity, even though he filed an affidavit supporting Jesse's position. I don't think Mona will call any of the Carr children, other than possibly Rand, because that could be disastrous, and she knows it. The bottom line is, we can't do anything about the format of the trial, but I think we can work within that frame-work, and we ought to be in a better position than Mona. But who knows? Mona might have a surprise for us."

Rod agreed, "I think you are right. I think it is look-ing good. I've gone over your game plan of how to present the case, and even your outline of questions to be asked by the Luke Green team, although they are good enough lawyers to know what to ask and what not to ask. It all looks good to me. The only thing that makes me nervous is that Luke himself has another trial conflict and can't be there. But I think he's done the first and most important thing, in having taken Mr. Carr's deposition, which will be our lead-off video witness, and I think the other members of the team will do a good job."

"I'm obviously sorry about Luke's absence also. He's the one I really hired for this job. But it is just not to be. I still believe it should go all right. We've done our homework. I have done all this detailed outlining, which should be a tremendous help to our team, and they are fully knowledgeable about the background and the facts. And, of course, you and I will be there. I've still got a few more things to do. Hope I don't have to deal with the Executive Committee again before trial. I know they aren't happy, but we have no choice. See you later," Ted concluded, as he shut down his folder and the two returned to their offices.

In the meantime, Mona Shadduck was meeting with Jesse Carr. "Now, Jesse, are you committed to going through with this trial?" Mona asked.

"Don't have much choice, do we? I feel like we have to go through with it, even though I'm not feeling so good. I've had some tests my doctor's handling, hope they come out fine, but I really don't feel good at all. And I hate to put Zander through it, but I'm not one to back down. What's happened was not right. I should have been the one from the beginning, and that lawyer got himself put in. But my question to you is, can we win? We ought to win, but what do you think?" Jesse Carr asked.

"Anything can happen in a lawsuit, Jesse. We are behind the eight ball with Zander's deposition, but our strong point is that it is in everybody's best interest for a family member, a brother, to handle Zander's affairs, not a lawyer who just did some paperwork that happens to have gotten himself included as an alternate rep for Zander. Even if the Judge thinks Zander lacks competency now, the downhill on dementia can be steep, and there is no proof he was incompetent when he executed your papers. We have affidavits on file by the Carr children, and some others, that support you, even though it looks like some of the Carr children are having second thoughts. If they don't turn against you at the hearing, it could still look like there's a united front to back you as the one in charge, and if the Judge thinks you are the right person for the job, he can find a way to rule for you. We've just got to convince him it makes no sense for Ted Born to serve in this critical role where a family member is needed. It could go either way. Are you still determined to go to trial?" Mona asked.

"I think so, but Rand tells me he is going to have separate counsel. Somebody has gotten it in his head that he could be disinherited under Zander's Will - the last one Ted Born drew up - if he opposes that Will, and he's worried. So, he will be doing what his new lawyer tells him. He's already explained it and apologized to me. But it's a helluva thing to do to me here at the last minute, 'specially since he's the one that talked me into doing this in the first place. And now I'm here holding the bag, and I don't feel like I'm getting the support of the family I ought to be getting," Jesse complained.

"You don't think Rand has turned on you, do you? I would like to talk to him, but I have to arrange it with his new lawyer, and the new lawyer said he wasn't ready to allow that, still had a lot of work to do to get up to speed on the case, but I didn't sense any overt hostility. There would be nothing wrong with *you* calling Rand and feeling him out. It's just that I, as a lawyer, cannot talk directly to the client of another lawyer without going through his lawyer. I'm stymied right now, but you are not," Shadduck advised.

"Okay. I might do that. Haven't seen much of Rand lately - used to see him almost every day when we first got started on this project, after John died," Jesse said.

"All right. Let's talk about the case, and your testimony," Mona said.

"Can we do this tomorrow or another time, Mona? I just don't feel like it right now," Jesse requested. Mona acceded, although she had set aside this time for that purpose. They would need to reschedule.

On the appointed day, the parties all assembled in the Probate Courtroom for the trial. All members of the Carr family were there, Shadduck representing only Jesse Carr, with Jason Smith representing all the Carr heirs except Rand, and Rand with his separate counsel, Bill Moulton. Ted Born was represented by the team of H.T. Gideon, Tilly Cole, and Barry Goodloe. Mr. Carr's brokerage firm was represented by Will Chambers, and his bank was represented by Tay Messer. Some of those in the courtroom had been formally named as parties in litigations, either in the Circuit Court or in the Probate Court, and others, like the Carr family represented by Jason Smith, had asked to intervene, and Probate Judge Justin Holcomb was liberal in allowing interventions. Mr. Carr was present, brought into the courtroom in a wheelchair, Jesse and his wife Candace were present, and Jesse with Mona Shadduck sat at the defendant counsel table, while Ted Born and his team sat at the plaintiff counsel table. Other attorneys and their clients sat on benches or chairs inside the railing separating litigants from spectators, but a few parties and lawyers chose to sit outside the railing, not expecting to participate actively.

Judge Holcomb called the Court to order while all in attendance rose and stood at attention, and then he motioned for all to take their seats. Although Born's team was prepared with an opening statement, Judge Holcomb announced, "Ladies and Gentlemen, the Court is generally familiar with the positions and contentions of the parties from previous hearings and filings, and this being a non-jury case, I am going to dispense with opening statements in the interest of time, so that we can get on with the presentation of evidence, as the evidence is what will determine my decision in this case. Mr. Born has filed the motion for instructions which initiated this case, and so he stands in the position of plaintiff. So, we will now hear the evidence he wishes to present. Please proceed."

H. T. Gideon rose, and said, "Your Honor, we would like first to play for the Court the video deposition of Alexander Carr. The sound video began to be played, showing Mr. Carr in his chair in his living room answering questions, after being sworn in. As the video began, Mr. Carr, seated at his counsel table, loudly asked: "Who is that talking?" Mona whispered something to him and gave him the "be quiet" signal with finger against her lips. Mr. Carr could not see the video because of his macular degeneration, and he apparently did not recognize his own voice. Judge Holcomb could be seen making a note on a pad in front of him. As the video continued, with Mr. Carr praising Ted Born and referring to Born as his attorney and that he would never replace Born, did not remember signing any documents replacing him, and not remember ever signing any documents naming Jesse, the Judge could be seen actively writing notes on his pad. The Judge raised his eyebrows quite noticeably when Mr. Carr in the video began having problems remembering who Mona Shadduck was, who was purporting to represent him in the proceedings. Mr. Carr continued to reinforce his confidence in Ted Born and his belief that

Born was his attorney, that he had never dismissed him, and he believed Born was a good person to protect his interests as his attorney-in-fact. The best he could say about Jesse was that Jesse had offered to help him and that he was glad to have his help, but obviously he meant general help, not in a fiduciary capacity. The testimony got better and better as Luke Green's questioning came to an end, and Will Chambers, for the brokerage firm and Tay Messer for the bank asked their questions. The Judge seemed surprised at the relatively few questions Mona Shadduck asked Mr. Carr, which in no way contradicted any of Mr. Carr's strong testimony on direct examination.

There was a break called at the conclusion of the video, and during the break Ted walked over toward Mr. Carr, where he had been joined by Jesse's wife Candace - Jesse himself and Mona having left the counsel table during the break. Ted leaned over, extended his right hand toward Mr. Carr and gently touched him on the shoulder with his left hand. This infuriated Candace who apparently saw herself as Zander's protector, and she rose from her chair and angrily said, "Get away from here! You are not welcome. You are interfering and insulting him!" Not wishing to get into a confrontation in the courtroom, Ted looked silently at Candace for a moment, then quietly moved back, just saying to Mr. Carr that he would see him later. Ted then realized that all in the courtroom had stopped whatever they were doing and were watching. Judge Holcomb was not in the courtroom during the break and did not see the confrontation, though his law clerk was there and saw it.

When the Court reconvened after the break, H.T. Gideon called Ted to the witness stand. He asked Born to relate his relationship with Mr. Carr. Ted told how Mr. Carr had called him some 25 years earlier to request his representation of him on an IRS matter on which he had gotten very good results, that Mr. Carr had thereafter solicited his counsel on a many matters over the years, including his estate planning. He said he or his firm had prepared about 12 different versions of Mr. Carr's will over the years, plus a number of interim codicils to each will, as well as various updated powers of attorney and, in more recent years, a living Trust document. He related how Mr. Carr had taken time to consider whom he should name as the alternate to his brother John, who was his primary attorney-in-fact, Trustee and designated Executor.

"And did he make and advise you of his choice of alternate?" asked Gideon.

"Yes, he did. He called and asked me if I would be the alternate," Born responded.

"Had you expected that?"

"Not at all. In fact, I was a little flustered, and asked him 'why me?'"

"And did he explain why?" asked Gideon.

"Yes, he said he had come to trust me and that he did not know of anyone else that would be suitable," Born replied.

"Did he say why no one else was suitable?" Gideon asked.

At that point, Shadduck rose and said, "I object, Your Honor. What he told Mr. Born is hearsay, and there is no way to verify the accuracy of what he might say was told him."

Gideon responded, "Your Honor, this is not at all hearsay, because Mr. Born was a party to the attorney-client conversation and would be relating what he heard with his own ears, not something second-hand. Besides, Ms. Shadduck has Mr. Carr with her in the courtroom and she will be free to call Mr. Carr as a witness to verify or contradict Mr. Born's testimony about what he said."

Judge Holcomb made his ruling, "I agree that this is not hearsay. Objection overruled. The witness can answer the question."

Born: "He said he did not want to choose one of his children because it might be taken as a sign that he favored one of them more than the others or had more confidence in one than he had in the others. Then he said, 'And I could never name Jesse as my alternate. I don't want him ever to have anything to do with my financial affairs.' He said he had thought of naming his CPA but felt he was too old and might not survive Mr. Carr or be able to handle the responsibilities when the time came. Finally, he said 'I have come to know you, and I trust your integrity and your judgment.'"

Gideon: "How did you answer him?"

Born: "I told him I was honored that he would want to name me as his alternate, but I needed to think about that and would be back in touch. I in fact did think about it, long and hard, and I really did not want to take on this role because I was a lawyer, and that was my focus. Still, he obviously wanted me to agree, and I decided it was unlikely I would ever have to serve, because Mr. Carr seemed in good health and his brother John was apparently in good health, and I knew it was possible he would change his mind anyway and it would just be a moot question. So, I agreed as an accommodation to my client, to be able to put a name in a blank space in the paperwork, thinking it would probably never be an issue, and for nearly 25 years it was not an issue."

Gideon: "Did he explain why he felt he could not name his brother Jesse as an alternate?"

Born: "Not at that time, except for saying they did not get along. I did not ask him at that time for a fuller explanation, because it was something personal with him, and none of my business."

Gideon: "Did you, at any later time, have occasion to discuss the matter of an alternate with Mr. Carr?"

Born. "Yes, I think virtually every time he did a revision of his will, the subject would come up, and he was adamant that Jesse must never have anything to do with his financial matters, and in fact he made me vow that I wouldn't let it happen." Then he added, "That's the only reason I am here. I made a vow, which Mr. Carr insisted on, that I would never let Jesse get involved in his financial affairs. I probably should not have made such a vow, and I wouldn't have, if I had thought ahead and realized that something like this might happen."

Gideon: "What do you mean by 'something like this'?"

Born: "I mean that when his brother John died, I entered on my responsibilities under the power of attorney, inventorying and securing his assets, dealing with arrangements with his staff and sitters, and trying to connect with all of his children – which never happened. And then, Jesse came to my office and confronted me with a new power of attorney he had somehow gotten Mr. Carr to sign, displacing me and naming himself as the responsible party – the one thing Mr. Carr had felt so strongly about, that he never wanted to happen. I had made a vow to him, several times, in fact, and now I was being tested, and I realized it was not solely within my power to prevent Jesse from taking over. It was something a Court would have to decide."

Gideon: "So, how did you decide to deal with this situation?"

Born: "Prayed about it, talked with my partner Rod Olson about it, and decided to put it in the hands of this Court, asking for its oversight. I never wanted the job in the first place, and if the Court determined the new power of attorney was valid, I would accept it and honor it, and gladly walk away with a clear conscience that I had done everything I could do to fulfill my vow. And if the answer was that the power of attorney was not executed knowingly and with full volition of Mr. Carr, then I would likewise accept that, and carry out my responsibilities to Mr. Carr as promised."

Gideon: "Mr. Born, did you file this request for instructions in order to hang on so that you could bill for a lot of fees for your services?"

Born: "That was not even a factor. As I said, I didn't want the job at all, whatever the fees might be. But if I took the job, I would only be billing at my usual hourly rate, and those fees would be only a very small portion of what my overall annual fee billings would be – not enough to influence my actions here, even if I had been thinking in those terms – which I wasn't. I just want justice for Mr. Carr."

Mr. Gideon asked other questions designed to show that Born was qualified to handle the job, and then he concluded his examination. Ms. Shadduck was the only other attorney that had any questions.

Ms. Shadduck: "Mr. Born are you aware now, and were you aware when John Carr died, that, based on the size of Mr. Carr's estate you could possibly have charged a fee of $900,000 or more?"

Born: "I never thought in those terms because we don't bill that way. We bill by the hour. I just knew I would not only have to do the work required of me, but I would need to make rather frequent visits of a social nature to Mr. Carr's home for which I could not bill in good conscience."

Shadduck: "Do you understand that it is possible for someone like Mr. Carr to have a change of mind about who is best suited to be an alternate?"

Born: "Of course. That's why I asked this Court to decide whether that was what happened in this case."

Shadduck: "Mr. Born, can you understand that as a person gets older and has some physical infirmities, that he might decide he needs to have a family member to handle his financial matters along with other issues relative to his care, even if in younger years he had been thinking in terms of an outsider, like his lawyer?"

Born: "Possible, but unlikely in this case."

Shadduck: "What's so different about this case?"

Born: "First, Mr. Carr was the soul of politeness and a stickler for doing everything the 'right' way. If he had had a change of mind, he would have told me that first, and would not have done it behind my back and had Jesse deliver the paperwork to me. In fact, I was with him just the day before the 'new' power of attorney papers were dated, and he never mentioned any intention to displace me. Second, as Mr. Carr testified in his deposition that we all heard earlier today, he had no intention of displacing me, and still does not, nor does he remember signing any paperwork that would have had that effect. Third, Mr. Carr was so passionately opposed to Jesse's service over such a long period of time, nearly 25 years, even making me vow to prevent it, that it is unlikely those strong feelings could be so easily set aside, at least without discussing it with me first."

Shadduck: "Mr. Carr is here with us in the courtroom. Will you look him in the face and tell him you think he was mentally incompetent to sign the power of attorney document he signed? Will you turn and say that to his face?"

Born: "I would only say that Mr. Carr was very vulnerable because of a combination of physical and memory problems, given his age, his nearly blind eyesight impairment, his arthritis and mobility problems, his prediabetic condition, his heart problems and his memory problems, and I can understand how a trusting person under those disabilities might sign a document put in front of him without fully understanding its import. I think there will be evidence presented by experts as to Mr. Carr's mental competence, and I will leave it at that."

After a few more questions, Shadduck sat down, and it was time for the next witness. This time Barry Goodloe, the probate specialist on the Luke green team, called to the witness stand Dr. Weinstein, the neuropsychiatrist who had examined Mr. Carr. He displayed his test results, explaining that Mr. Carr's eyesight prevented him from filling out his own form but that a physician's assistant had filled in his answers to questions read to him. The results showed that he scored in very low percentiles in a series of tests, indicative of mental impairment. He described his attempts to communicate with Mr. Carr and how the interactions strongly suggested mental and memory impairment. He was asked about Mr. Carr's deposition, and he said that, while Mr. Carr's short-term memory was almost completely gone, he still had a fair amount of his long-term memory and that it was obvious he still retained positive feelings about and confidence in Ted Born, validating his choice of Born as his alternate over many years when he could have, but did not, change his mind. He was asked to comment on the test results of Dr. Tercelli, and he said Tercelli's respective objective results were very similar, consistent with his own, and he noted that Dr. Tercelli had hedged in his opinion as to Mr. Carr's competency. He said he thought it would be quite a stretch to conclude he was mentally competent to execute legal documents, considering the objective test results, even aside from the other problems.

The trial was recessed for the day after the testimony of the neuropsychiatrist, to be reconvened the next day. The team of Born's lawyers convened at Luke Green's law offices, absent Luke, to discuss the events of the day. Rod Olson spoke up, "As an observer not on the front lines of this trial, I have to say it couldn't have gone much better. Leading off with the deposition of Mr. Carr was definitely the right move. It showed clearly what Mr. Carr's thinking and attitude are, as of today, impaired or not, and he clearly is still in your corner, Ted. Then, I thought Ted's examination went really well. You were credible, and your testimony about why he wanted you and did NOT want Jesse, was powerful; and Mona didn't lay a glove on you on cross-examination. Our psychiatrist was also very credible, and Mona could not shake him, either. So, what do we have left that we still need to do?"

Tilly Cole spoke up, "I will be calling Jesse the first thing tomorrow morning, as an adverse and hostile witness, and then Rand, also as an adverse witness. We are prepared to call Kate, and maybe we also need to call you, Rod, because you heard Mr. Carr saying he didn't want Jesse and you could back up Ted's testimony. I notice the Judge was taking a lot of notes of testimony very favorable to us, so I think we definitely have an edge. I just don't know what Mona can do when her turn comes.

At Mona's office, a different conversation was taking place. "Now, look," Mona was saying. "Let's face it. This was not a great day for us, but just remember this is Born's turn, and you expect him to be scoring some points. We still have our expert coming up, and, Jesse, you and Rand can tell your stories. Wish Rand didn't have separate counsel, because that inserts a new level of uncertainty. Just remember, also, that if we lose, we always knew we might lose in this Probate Court, we can always appeal."

"But Mona," said Jesse. 'If we appeal, can we get our original Circuit Court case reactivated, putting Born on the defensive and subjecting him to personal damages?"

"I'm not sure we can," answered Mona. "If Born wins in the Probate Court, he will probably be protected from liability, because the law presumes that Born's position was reasonable if he wins in the Probate Court, and that would shield him from liability for raising the issue as to the validity of your power of attorney – even if the Probate verdict was later overturned on appeal. I am not sure about that, but it is like a grand jury, I think. If a grand jury indicts someone for a crime, that action shields an accuser from liability for falsely accusing the person of a crime, and from false arrest. This would probably work the same way. We will cross that bridge when we get to it. Any inclination to try to settle?"

"No," said Jesse. "I don't see a way to compromise. I'm not going to work with Born, and he's not going to work with me. We've taken it this far, so let's see it through. I wish I was feeling better. I'm losing some of my instinct to fight, just feel lousy, and I've got some problems I don't even want to talk about. Let's just see it through."

Court resumed the next morning, and Judge Holcomb, said, "Please call your next witness." Tilly Cole rose and said, "Your Honor, we call Jesse Carr as an adverse and hostile witness."

Jesse Carr ambled toward the witness stand with some papers in his hand and took his seat. After being sworn in, Tilly began asking him questions. After getting him to identify himself for the record, Tilly began the substance of her interrogation.

"Mr. Carr, you have had a strained relationship with your brother, Alexander Carr for some years, have you not?" Tilly asked.

"I wouldn't say that. He went his way, and I went mine. We had some ups and downs, but that happens in every family." Jesse answered.

Cole: "Did you go for months or even years without seeing or speaking to him?"

Jesse: "I don't remember. Don't think it was that long, at least usually."

Cole: "Did you sometimes give large parties and not invite your brother Zander to them?"

Jesse: "I don't remember. Might have happened once or twice."

Cole: "You were in a commercial business once, weren't you? What happened to that business?

Jesse: "I sold it."

Cole: "Was it a profitable business?"

Jesse: "I was trying to get there; it was a startup."

Cole: "Did you sell it to avoid bankruptcy?"

Jesse: "I wouldn't say that. Just didn't think it was right for me, and I sold it."

Cole: "Did you have a falling out with your brother Zander over what he thought was a bad investment?"

Jesse: "I wouldn't call it a falling out. That was a long time ago. I don't remember."

Cole: "When your brother John died, it had been at least months since you had spoken to or seen your brother Zander, had it not?"

Jesse: "I don't remember. He was still my brother."

Cole: "But you would agree he got along a lot better with your brother John than with you, and John was very close to him?"

Jesse: "They were close, but we were all brothers."

Cole: "Did you and your nephew Rand have a conversation about your becoming Zander's power of attorney holder after John's death?"

Jesse seemed to be moving his papers back and forth and looking down at them as he answered questions. He answered," Maybe. Nobody's business. Don't remember."

Cole: "Who came up with the idea of hiring Greg Tween?"

Jesse: "That was Rand's idea. I didn't think much of him, not a fighter. We got somebody else."

Cole: "Who did you get to prepare the power of attorney you took to Zander to sign?"

Jesse: "Not sure. Some lawyer."

Cole: "Did Zander tell you to draw up a new power of attorney and put your name on it as the attorney-in-fact?"

Jesse: "Maybe. I don't remember. I knew Zander needed help. I wanted to help him."

Cole: "Did Zander ever tell you he wanted to replace Mr. Born?"

Jesse: "It's been a long time ago." He looked down at his sheets of paper and said, "I know he needed help, needed a family member."

Ted was watching this questioning with great interest, noticing particularly how Jesse was increasingly looking at the three sheets of paper in his hand. He tapped Tilly Cole on the arm and whispered, "Tilly, ask him to let you see the papers in his hands. He keeps looking at them and seems to be using them as prompters."

Cole: "Mr. Carr, you seem to have some papers in your hand that you are referring to. May I see them?" Jesse sheepishly handed over the three sheets of paper. It appeared that there were some key words written in the extreme left-hand side of each sheet, apparently so that he could slide them back and forth and read the notes without having to fold them over or shuffle them very much.

Cole: "Mr. Carr, who told you to make these notes and bring them with you when you testified?"

Jesse looked at Mona who had a frown on her face. "I just did it," he said.

Cole: "Did anyone tell you to do it or suggest that you do it?"

Jesse: "I 'm not sure. Can we take a break?"

Cole: "We haven't been going very long, Mr. Carr. I would ask the Court to allow us to continue until we finish this line of questioning."

"Please proceed," said Judge Holcomb looking up from the notes he had been furiously making on his pad.

"Your Honor, I would like to mark the three sheets of paper that Mr. Carr just handed us as the next exhibit in order, and I offer them in evidence," said Cole.

"Hearing no objection, they are admitted," said the Judge.

Cole: "Mr. Carr, I see notes written in the left-hand margins that say things like, 'don't remember,' 'Rand,' with a line drawn through it, 'his idea.' And a lot of others I have not deciphered yet. Why didn't you tell us in the beginning that you would be testifying from these notes, using them as prompters"?

Jesse: "Well, I'm 86 years old, and my memory is not as good as it used to be. I need these notes. I'm doing the best I can."

Cole: "You mean, you are doing the best you can to destroy Mr. Born and his reputation and to try to get a big judgment against him just because he tried to do what Mr. Carr demanded of him?"

Jesse: "Well, I don't see it that way. Zander needs me and family and that lawyer's messing things up."

Cole: "You mean you would try to help Zander by mortgaging his house, don't you?"

Jesse: "You make it sound bad. We needed the money to pay Mona, who's helping him."

Cole: "You mean she's helping you get control of Zander's money, don't you?"

Jesse: "I think that's helping Zander."

Cole: "How much of Zander's money have you already paid Mona? And how much do you still owe her?"

Jesse: "I don't know. I can't remember those things. I'm just trying to help Zander."

Cole: "And you said in one of your emails to Rand that you were going to make 'a whole lot of changes' once you got control of things. What kind of changes were you planning to make?"

Jesse: "I don't remember, don't remember any email like that."

Cole, showing him a copy of the email, "Do you recognize this email now, Mr. Carr? By the way, you never produced this in discovery; we got it only through discovery directed to Rand. Looks like you were planning to change the distributions under the will. You were always resentful that Zander didn't leave you as much as he left John and each of his own children, weren't you?"

"I don't remember," Jesse said.

After a few more questions, Tilly Cole suggested to the Court that it might be well to take a break, as Jesse Carr's face was flushed and it was not clear he could continue, and the Judge, still writing furiously, looked up and announced a 15-minutee recess. Ted congratulated Tilly on a job well done and said, "Tilly, you have done a great job destroying any credibility this guy might otherwise have. I don't think I would ask him another question, and I don't think Mona will be inclined to call him back to the stand as her witness. I think it best to let things lie where they are." All on Born's team agreed.

Just then, Rand's separate counsel, Bill Moulton, came up to Born and said, "Ted, I just want you to know that we – Rand and I – don't have anything to do with these sleazeballs."

"I appreciate that, Bill, and I wish we could work with you instead of against you. Talk with Rand and see if he won't join his brothers and sister to put an end to all this, maybe influence Jesse as well." He agreed to talk with Rand.

The trial continued, but everyone knew that it was all over.

CHAPTER NINETEEN

AFTER THE TRIAL

A heavy weight was lifted from Ted's shoulders. The trial had gone as well as he could have hoped. By the assessments of everyone, the result would be a huge win for Born. But there had not yet been any opinion issued. The Judge had taken the case under advisement and was apparently taking his time.

In the meantime, the communication between Born and the Carr heirs had gotten looser and freer, as they all were anticipating a Born win. Still, there was no movement from Jesse or Mona Shadduck for any kind of settlement. Ted had expected that, in the interlude between a trial that had gone well for him and the time when an actual decision would be rendered, his opposition would consider that this would be a good time to initiate settlement discussions. Certainly, Jesse would be in a much less favorable posture to negotiate in an environment where a decision adverse to him had passed from an expectancy to a concrete reality.

Yet there was total silence from Jesse and Mona. The frustration was magnified by Ted's inability to see Zander Carr or to do any of the things relative to his care that a good power of attorney holder should be doing, because he as yet had no legal authorization to do any of those things, without a Court Order – only continuing his management of the Trust funds.

Then one day he got a telephone call from Bruce Carr. "Ted, you might not have gotten the word yet, but Uncle Jesse is in the hospital. I thought you ought to know."

"What's wrong, Bruce?" Ted asked.

"Not sure," Bruce responded. "He can't have visitors. Candace isn't saying anything, nor Mona. But I gather he's a mess."

"I'm sorry to hear that, Bruce. He was my adversary, and the tone of his accusations against me were – I thought – vicious and beyond the pale. But I never wished him any harm. I hope he can recover from whatever his medical problem is. Thanks for calling." Born said. Then he called Rod Olson and asked him to come by for a chat. "Rod, I just got a phone call from Bruce Carr saying Jesse Carr is in the hospital. Sounds serious, but he doesn't have any details, or at least he says he doesn't. I wonder if Jason Smith has any more information. As the Carr family attorney, I would think he ought to know something, even though he isn't representing Jesse in our litigation. I think I will give him a ring."

"Hi, Jason," Born said. "I just heard that Jesse Carr is in the hospital, but I don't have a clue as to what the problem is or how serious. I hope it isn't too bad. You know I don't wish him any harm."

"Ted, I don't have the details either, but I think it is pretty bad. Just reading between the lines, I don't think he's going to expire in the next day or two, but the long-range prospects don't seem to be too good. I think he's basically out of the picture, legally," Jason opined.

"Then, who's going to be calling the shots on his side of the case?" Born asked.

"I don't think anybody is going to step up and try to take over as long as he's still breathing, and, as far as I know, he could keep going for a while. I just don't know enough to say. I doubt if Rand would try to take charge, even though he is Jesse's alternate under the `new power of attorney,' a fact we haven't thought much about. But Rand has enough sense to know he and Jesse are on the losing side, and he at least partially broke from Jesse during the trial," Jason offered.

"Well, we are truly in limbo right now, then. We have no Court order. There has been no move toward settlement, and now Jesse is incapacitated. We are stymied, can't do anything, it seems. Let me know if you get any further information you can share. Many thanks," Ted concluded the conversation. Turning to Rod, who had been listening to the conversation via speakerphone, Ted said, "What do you make of it, Rod?"

"I'm trying to get a handle on it, Ted. I guess it is possible that we haven't heard anything from Jesse or his lawyer because he's been so preoccupied with medical problems that he's just put this case out of his mind. Certainly, if he has some sort of terminal illness, at his age 86, it essentially moots this whole litigation – except for the possibility that Rand would try to carry it on, which I think is remote. I've been hoping for a resolution sooner, rather than later, so that it would at least get the Executive Committee off our backs. You would think the EC would be delighted the trial went so well, but they weren't in the courtroom to witness it. There is still no written decision, and they want it settled, and want us to get out. If anything bad happened to Jesse at this time, it could cast a spotlight on the case, which the EC wouldn't like. Maybe I could check with Judge Holcomb's law clerk and provide a preliminary report about Jesse, and maybe we could get a little feedback as to where the Judge stands with his opinion," Rod suggested.

"I think you should do that, Rod. It might help a little to know whether an opinion is imminent or not," Ted advised. Rod said he would follow up.

A while later, Rod came back into Ted's office. "I've just had a chat with the Judge's law clerk," reported Rod. "The law clerk was interested to find out about Jesse's hospitalization. He said something to the effect that he wondered whether Jesse could deal with the lawsuit if he was still hospitalized when the opinion and order came out. There was something in the way he said it that made me feel like the opinion and order would be coming soon, but he did not actually say that. He asked me if I thought post-judgment mediation would be helpful on the question of attorney fees and any settlement of the possibility of an appeal, and I told him I thought it might be helpful, that it couldn't hurt. So, we might be getting a mediation order as well as a decision on the merits."

"Very interesting, Rod. I agree that some mediation would be good, probably should have had it long ago, but Mona was so sure she was going to win in the Circuit Court that it probably would not have done any good to try – at least until we got that issue behind us with the Supreme Court's mandamus order. There really isn't anything much we can do until the Court renders its decision, or until Jesse's status changes." Ted rubbed his chin and sat thinking as Rod excused himself.

Three days later, Ted and Rod received the long-awaited decision of the Probate Court! With fingers clumsily numb with anticipation, Ted opened the envelope and found an extensive Court opinion finding that Alexander Carr had been under undue influence while in a mentally and physically vulnerable state when he signed the paperwork presented to him by Jesse, that he had no intention to replace Ted Born as his attorney-in-fact, nor as his Trustee or potential executor under his will. The Court Order held that the estate planning documents of Alexander Carr, as they stood before Jesse's intervention, would govern the future status of Mr. Carr's estate, and Ted Born was recognized by the Court as the legal and properly constituted attorney-in-fact, Trustee and potential Executor, and the parties were admonished and enjoined from participating in any attempted modification of Zander's estate planning documents. The Court ordered mandatory mediation of attorney fees and possible settlement of any appeal options. Accompanying the Order was an opinion evaluating the evidence in the case, which was scathingly critical of Jesse Carr and his credibility, among other things.

"Wow! A slam dunk for our side! It's good to know we won, and decisively won! I'm not sure anything can compensate for the sheer agony I have gone through - probably shaved a few years off my life – but now I feel vindicated. But even more, Mr. Carr has been vindicated in that his carefully constructed estate-planning wishes are going to be honored," Ted told himself. The Judge had appointed a mediator as a part of his order, not leaving it to the parties to agree on one. And so, the stage was set for the final resolution of the litigation. Ted called Rod, who also had just opened the packet of papers containing the Court's rulings. "I'm still reading," Rod said, but it looks like a 'Glory Hallelujah' result! Congratulations, Ted!" Ted told him to finish reading and to think about the next legal step, saying he would be back in touch but needed to make a visit to Mr. Carr.

Ted headed for the elegant mansion where the philanthropist lived whose wishes and plans had so consumed him in the months just past. He took a couple of copies of the Court's Order with him in case the butler refused him entry into Mr. Carr's home. But Mr. Robbins the butler courteously greeted him, was interested in the Court Order, and said loudly to the cook, "The Judge has said Mr. Born is in charge again. I'm taking him up to see Mr. Carr now." Ted introduced himself to the sitter who was situated in a chair in the corner, and then greeted Mr. Carr with an extended hand and pat on the shoulder, "I'm back, Mr. Carr, and I hope I can safely come back to check with you a lot more often now. How are you doing?"

"Well, Ted, you know how it is. I'm a hundred years old, and I just don't feel good. The doctor doesn't seem to be helping," he told Born.

"Do you know anything about Jesse? Have you heard from him?" Ted asked.

"No, he comes sometimes. I guess he's all right," he said.

"Did you know he was in the hospital?"

"Hospital? No. What's wrong?" He seemed surprised, but more curious than concerned.

"We don't know," Ted said. "Don't even know which hospital. If it's anything serious, you might not see him for a while. But I will always be available. Your butler/chauffeur, Mr. Robbins, has all my contact information, and so does your cook, and I will make sure we put it on a piece of paper or an index card and tape it to your desk so all your sitters will have access as well. Another thing: You remember your accountant, Joe Henaker? Jesse fired him and replaced him with one of Rand's friends. My guess is that you would like to have him back as your accountant. If so, I'll call and reinstate him."

"I like Joe. Haven't seen him lately. I need him - taxes, you know," Mr. Carr responded.

"I'll call Joe, and I need to call some other people, too. I will be back, and do let me know if you need anything in the meantime."

Ted called Joe Henaker, told him about the Court Order, and asked if he would get back into monitoring and seeing that the household staff got paid and that the social security taxes and other matters were properly handled. Joe had not yet heard about the Court Order, but he was delighted. Ted told him he would contact the Jesse-appointed CPA and ask him to turn over all his records and paperwork to Joe. He then sent a copy of the Court Order and Opinion to the fund raiser for St. Bartholomew's, with a simple note that said, "I thought you might be interested in this." He sent another copy to Zander's concierge Doctor. Ted also contacted Mr. Carr's brokerage firm and his bank to make sure they were updated. Then he called Jason Smith. Jason congratulated him, said he had seen a copy of the Judge's Order and thought it was all powerful stuff, well done, and he had shared the information with all the Carr heirs except Rand, who would be getting it directly from his own separate counsel. The Carr heirs whom Smith represented were all satisfied. He told Ted that he had learned Jesse's medical situation was quite serious, but he said he was not at liberty to say anything more.

Having done what was necessary to reestablish his authority in handling Mr. Carr's affairs in accordance with Judge Holcomb's rulings, Ted got together with Rod. "Rod, here's where we are: The Probate Judge has ruled for us decisively. He's validated our documents and thrown out Jesse's. This would seem to have effectively mooted the case that Jesse and Mona filed in the Circuit Court, although it technically remains pending. Jesse is in the hospital with apparently a bad prognosis, but I don't have any details on that. However, it would seem that, whatever enthusiasm he had for this lawsuit would be gone as he deals with his medical condition – and with the inability to pay Mona to handle any probably futile appeal. That just leaves these remaining issues: First, how much do we bill in legal fees, and do we need Court approval to get them paid? Second, what fees should I charge for my Trustee and attorney-in-fact services going forward? Third, Mona is going to want to be paid, and how do we deal with that, assuming she is now ready to settle the case? I guess we should consider whether to demand, and perhaps sue her for, damages for putting us through a groundless Circuit Court lawsuit. Let's talk this out."

"All right, here are some thoughts. First, yes, unless we get a settlement where all parties agree on the figures, I think we need to get Court approval of our attorney fees," counseled Rod. "We are talking about a lot more money than we ever contemplated, even applying just our normal hourly billing rates, and this has been a very contentious litigation. We need Court approval so that you are not accused of violating your fiduciary duties to Mr. Carr by making your own unilateral decision to pay yourself with his money. The same thing goes for your Trustee/power-of-attorney fees going forward. And of course, we need Court approval of the fees that Luke Green's firm will be charging. The Court needs to pre-approve all those fees for the same reason. Then you won't have a fight in the future about your fees. As far as Mona's fees are concerned, some of them have been paid, and I know it hurts to pay her anything more after her misconduct in hurling outrageous accusations at you. However, looking at this from a strictly lawyerly viewpoint, she is going to say she had an agreement with Jesse, who had apparently a genuine power of attorney that she did not draft (remember it was Greg Tween that drafted it before Jesse fired him and hired her), and she will say she in good faith relied on Jesse's authority – which the power of attorney on its face says she is entitled to do – and she expects to have her fees honored, even though the Court has retroactively invalidated Jesse's POA. Assuming she is willing to settle, and it does not seem like that she will have much choice now, I think you would be wise to put this whole nightmare behind you, agree to her fee, if you can't persuade her to reduce it, and look to the future. We need to consider an expert witness to express an opinion on our past fees and your future fees, if we can't reach universal agreement with everyone about that, in the mandatory mediation Judge Holcomb has ordered. Of course, if all the parties reach agreement in the mediation, then it won't be necessary to get an expert on the fees."

"I've been thinking along the same lines, Rod," Ted reflected. "It hurts to pay anything to that lawyer who so maliciously assailed me and smeared my name. It really hurts. But, in the first place, she did it in filed documents in this litigation, and that generally immunizes her from what would otherwise be defamatory. In any event, in the end, what good does it do me to let my trauma continue to dominate any part of my life after I've been vindicated?

I would just be prolonging the hurt, and I don't think it would help my feelings by depriving her of her fee. What good would that do me? We can ask her to reduce her fees, but if she won't, and if the Court approves them, we just need to pay them out of Mr. Carr's Trust funds and move on. Now, do you have someone in mind to serve as an expert on the fee issues?"

"I have a couple of thoughts, but let me check on conflicts and availability," Rod responded. We might not need an expert at this point if we can agree to the figures through mediation.

"That's fine, but, speaking of conflicts, I am concerned about Judge Holcomb's choice of a mandatory mediator in resolving the remaining issues – Braxton Bartley," Ted said. "I don't know Braxton well, and he seems like a fine person and has a good reputation as a lawyer. What gives me pause is the fact that he is a partner of Greg Tween, who was originally Jesse's lawyer in this case. I know Greg is not Jesse's lawyer anymore, and only briefly represented him. I'm also confident Judge Holcomb did not think about that partnership connection when he appointed Braxton. It is possible that Braxton is not aware of it, either, and likely Greg has never discussed it with him, as they are in a good-size firm, where you tend to lose track of what your partners are doing. I don't necessarily want to raise the issue unless you feel differently about it. I'm sure Judge Holcomb just appointed Braxton because he had a lot of confidence in his judgment and effectiveness. But what do you think?"

"I think you've assessed it just right. It probably would be a conflict that would disqualify Braxton if we raised it, but since I like the choice I think we should not raise the issue. After all, he's a mediator, not an arbitrator, and he can't make us agree to anything - he can only advise and nudge us all to get together on settlement. Do we even mention it to him this possible conflict?" Rod questioned.

"I think not, Rod. Mentioning it to him might make him feel obligated to recuse himself, which I don't think we want. Also, Judge Holcomb's Opinion and Order were so powerful that I think it supersedes and would override any possible favoritism toward the other side. In fact, unless Braxton seems openly hostile, which I don't expect, I would dismiss it as an issue *even if Braxton brings it up*," Ted counseled.

The phone rang. It was Braxton Bartley. "Hi, Ted. Long time, no see. As you might have guessed, I am calling you about this Carr case. I'm making my way through the opinion. Sounds like you had a strong case and got a resounding win. I guess my job is to try to settle the outstanding litigation. There's the possibility of appeal, and then there is the issue of fees, as well as that Circuit Court case hanging out there. I haven't talked with Mona yet, but I would think this is the kind of case that ought to be settled. I will need to see your time records; you can of course redact any attorney-client communications reflected in the records, and I will appreciate your providing me with a memo stating your position on your fees and Mona's. Of course, I will need the same thing from all the various law firms. As soon as I get this information from everybody, I will have a separate meeting with each of you and try to assess where we are. Does that sound OK?"

"That's exactly right, Braxton. It's just what I would expect, and you can count on us to cooperate. You will get our figures and memo, and I trust Mona will cooperate too. I guess you would intend to mediate the ongoing fees for my future services as well, would you not? It would be good to get that nailed down so that it would not be an issue down the road," Ted suggested.

"Yes, you are right. It looks like maybe your fees – or some of the Carrs' fears of your fees - might have been a big part of what instigated this litigation, so let's cut off at the pass any future potential issue about that. You can give me expert testimony on that, if you wish, but I'm not sure we need it. If all the Carrs agree, it doesn't matter. I'm beginning to have an idea of a proper figure already. But I will have separate conference with you and Mona and other counsel about all these things."

"Sounds fine, Braxton. We'll get to work," said Ted.

CHAPTER TWENTY

THE FIRM HAS ITS SAY

The parties made their submissions to mediator Braxton Bartley. The attorney fees had mounted up on all sides. Mona's fees sounded excessive to Ted and Rod, but it seemed futile to make an issue of it. Ted regretted that the cost of the litigation had had a negative impact on Mr. Carr's assets, but he did not feel responsible for it, and he felt Mr. Carr would have wanted him to fight to have his directives upheld and honored, even at a high cost. Braxton came to Ted toward the end of the negotiations and said, I have a figure in mind for your fees for future services as Trustee and under the power of attorney. It would be an annual fee, payable to you in monthly installments, or to your Firm. If you can agree, I think the Carr family heirs will all agree, and we can put this whole thing to bed."

Ted thought Braxton's figure was fair, perhaps even generous, except possibly for the unexpected issues that could always come up when dealing with expectant heirs who do not have possession of the assets now but know they are in line to get them at some future date. Both Ted and Braxton knew that, at Mr. Carr's age and with his health issues, Ted's services might be relatively brief, perhaps a matter of a few months, perhaps a matter of a few years. But then, Ted would be Executor of the estate and would be charged with overseeing the liquidation of the estate, the payment of estate taxes, and the distribution of assets, all of which would take a while. The compensation agreement would not apply to the settlement of the estate after Mr. Carr's death, as that would be a separate matter for the Probate Court to approve those fees. All things considered, Ted thought he should accept Braxton's figure, with the stipulation that the same compensation arrangement would apply to any successor Trustee if Ted should withdraw or be disqualified for any reason. The Carr family heirs agreed to the arrangement, and the settlement was approved by the Court. The Circuit Court litigation was also dismissed with prejudice, the Probate Court retaining jurisdiction to enter any further orders that might be necessary. All fees were paid in accordance with the settlement, Ted continued to be Trustee and holder of Mr. Carr's power of attorney, and all matters seemed to have been settled and put to rest.

It was early November when the settlement became final, with decisive vindication of Ted Born's posture relative to the litigation. The Firm's Executive Committee, as a part of its job of annually setting compensation for partners, undertook its year-end evaluation of each of the partners. Each partner was required to submit data showing hours worked, amounts billed to clients, the amounts collected, and comments about notable achievements or, in some cases, shortcomings and disappointments. Born was accustomed to filling out such forms; in fact, he had suggested the process originally while serving on the Executive Committee, in order to get away from overly subjective or superficial evaluations. He was especially happy to fill out the form this year because, in addition to the positive data relative to the Carr case, and its extraordinarily good results, he had had an overall excellent year on any objective financial basis. He recognized that, being 72 years old, he would be subject to a mandatory reduction in his participation in partnership earnings, which had begun when he had earlier reached age 65. As one of the Firm's most highly compensated lawyers, he had been at or near the pinnacle when he was 65 and, notwithstanding the gradual reductions in his partnership earnings percentages, he had continued to be well compensated, as the increased profitability of the firm offset, to a considerable degree, the automatic percentage reductions. The Firm also had a bonus system that was designed to reward any lawyer for outstanding achievements, over and above the assigned compensation arrangements.

Born was in excellent health, was energetic and looked much younger than his biological age. He felt and thrived on the exhilaration of winning and being able to look appreciative clients in the face after helping them survive difficult challenges. He had no thought other than to continue to practice law with passion and excellence and to feel the satisfaction that comes from just being a good lawyer. His plan was to continue to serve as Alexander Carr's Trustee during the upcoming calendar year, and his Trustee fees would be turned over to the Firm like any other income he might bring in, to be put into a common "pot" and distributed out to the partners, after deduction of expenses. Of course, he would continue to do work for his other clients as well. The Firm was like a family to Ted, and he could no more conceive of life without being an actively practicing lawyer in the Firm than he could imagine aimlessly lolling around on a beach somewhere, day after day.

There had been a parade of Firm lawyers who came by to congratulate Ted and Rod on their big win. Noticeably absent were members of the Executive Committee.

Following the submission of the annual evaluation forms, there was always an interview conducted by a member of the Executive Committee. It happened that Born's interview that year would be conducted by a partner who lived in another state, who had come into the Firm fairly recently via a merger of law practices of the two former firms. Ted did not know his interviewer well, nor did the interviewer, Adam Ford, know him well. They went over all the data and how it stacked up against other lawyers, and Ted made the point that he felt his performance justified a generous compensation arrangement, as well as a generous bonus. Ford was unresponsive to Ted's "brief" in support of his merit performance, and then looked down at the floor and said, "And what about conduct?" Born was taken aback by what seemed a strange question, and said, "I think my conduct has been exemplary. I have been decisively vindicated in a major case by a Court that heard all the evidence. I was faithful to my commitment to the client at great personal trauma, and it was a vindication not only of me but of the client's intentions and directions to me. No one has found me to have done anything unethical, and I think the legal bar has a higher regard for the Firm because I am here." Ford said nothing in response, but closed the interview and departed, presumably to conduct interviews with other partners. What a strange and unexpected encounter, Ted thought.

Later in December, there was a meeting of the Executive Committee, at which Adam Ford made his report. "I have studied the data for Ted Born and have interviewed him. He doesn't seem to have a clue that he has been a problem to the Firm this last year or two. We have wrestled with the fact that he undertook to act as a Trustee for a client while representing the client as a lawyer, which is a recipe for disaster, and, predictably, he got sued over it. Our malpractice carrier was all over us for permitting that to happen and told us the case needed to be settled immediately. We repeatedly directed Born to settle the case, and he kept putting us off, and putting us off again and again, and finally it went to trial. Fortunately, he won the case, and in his mind that makes everything all right. But now he plans to continue serving as Trustee, setting the stage for more trouble down the road, and I am concerned our malpractice carrier will cancel the coverage of the whole Firm. He is putting the entire firm at risk because he wants to take on a role that is verboten. He is a risk to the Firm. He's 72 years old and, yeah, I've heard he was a pretty good lawyer in his day, but his day has come and gone. I'm even afraid that he has lost his sense of perspective. Maybe he is developing dementia. I don't know, but regardless, I think he needs to go. He steadfastly refused to settle the case and get out of it, flouting the direct orders of this Committee."

"What about his objective productivity during the year, Adam?" asked Carl Heimat.

"It was good, in fact pretty impressive, but that is not the point. The point is that he is a loose cannon and is a danger to the Firm. I don't think we ought to give him any bonus. If you want to be very generous to him, you could do this: Give him no bonus, give him the choice of renouncing his trusteeship and staying with the Firm at reduced compensation, or if he wants to remain a Trustee, he will have to leave the Firm. That's my assessment," Ford reported.

There were discussions that followed. Some who really knew Born declared that, whatever else might be true, Born was a very bright and judicious person and a very productive lawyer, notwithstanding his age, and was responsible for founding the Firm's premier patent and trademark group, in addition to being a very versatile and highly productive lawyer.

Ford responded that Born's versatility might be a part of the problem, that if he were more focused in some one area of the law he might have better judgment as to how to handle dangerous cases. The Committee adjourned to consider the matter further. Ted Born was in his office, one floor away, dealing with clients and oblivious to the tenor of the meeting just concluded above him.

In early January, after all financial data for the Firm had been updated and considered, it was time for EC members to visit each partner's office and announce the firm's compensation decision respecting that partner. The Chair and a younger EC member knocked on Ted's door and then entered. After the "Hello" and "How-are-you" greetings, they got down to business. "Ted, the Executive Committee has decided that you will have to make a choice as to whether to stay with the Firm or continue as a Trustee for Mr. Carr. You cannot do both.

There will be a modest bonus for you for last year, but if you stay with the Firm, you'll receive reduced compensation at a rate comparable to a five- or six-year associate."

"Then you have my resignation," Ted said without hesitation. "If that is what the firm wants, it has been achieved. I have said over and over, after I reached the 'normal' retirement age of 65, that I would leave the Firm without hesitation any time the Firm wished me to do so. At those times, the Firm always said it needed me, so I stayed, and I have tried to continue to be an asset to the Firm. The Firm obviously feels differently now, and of course it is a different Firm, changing every year. So, my decision is to resign and leave, and I will not change my mind about that. However, I feel that the way this has been handled is insulting, and I request an opportunity to state my case to the entire Executive Committee."

"How long have you been with the Firm, Ted?"

"Forty-Eight years. It's been family to me. I've had the opportunity to grow and to benefit from my interaction with bright and well-educated lawyers whom I regarded as not just professionals, but good friends. It has been stimulating, and I am grateful that I could be nurtured in that environment and have had the opportunity to nurture others who have come along. I will miss it, but the world changes, and I know I have to change accordingly. It is time to say good-bye. Thank you for your time."

"You are entitled to be heard by the whole Committee. As you know, we almost never change our decisions, but you are entitled to be heard, if you wish," advised the Chairman.

CHAPTER TWENTY-ONE

BORN HAS HIS SAY

Ted Born entered the large conference room where the Executive Committee had assembled. After a few brief neutral remarks, the Chairman nodded for Ted to proceed.

"I want to thank all of you for coming to hear me, and I want to thank the Chairman for arranging it and for very generously saying that there would be no particular time limit on what I have to say. Nevertheless, I know that you are all busy lawyers with work to do and clients to take care of, and I will be mindful of the time and will try not to abuse your indulgence.

"I am here because I want you to know that my conduct which apparently gave rise to your concerns about me will forever stand in my own mind as the proudest single accomplishment of my 48-year tenure here. I am proud in part because I have been vindicated by our judicial system, but much more importantly because my efforts helped to ensure that a long-time client's estate planning wishes and directives have been honored at a time he was no longer able to fend for himself, and relatives for their own benefit were exploiting his vulnerable status and frustrating his clear wishes regarding his estate. I had been his lawyer for some 25 years, had consulted and worked with him on many legal matters, and he had confidence in me and my integrity and judgment. He asked me to be an alternate Executor, to back up his first choice who was his brother John. I did not seek or want that position, and I had to think about it before accepting it. I finally agreed to be listed as an alternate in the estate planning as an accommodation to him, as he said he had no one else who he thought was suitable. Above all other considerations, he adamantly and consistently stated that, under no circumstances was his other brother, Jesse, to have anything at all to do with his financial affairs. They were estranged, did not get along at all, and he left Jesse only a very modest inheritance. He made me swear I would never let Jesse have any involvement in his financial affairs. Later, when he executed a power of attorney and a living trust, he wanted to keep the same format, his brother John as the primary and I as the alternate. I knew of the intensity of his feelings about his brother Jesse, but I frankly never thought I would ever be confronted with having to carry out his admonitions and expectations; I thought his brother John could handle that very ably, if necessary.

"I would note that at the time I undertook this 'alternate' commitment, there seemed no concern in the Firm that it would be improper for me to serve in fiduciary capacities for this client while rendering legal services. I knew of instances where lawyers in the Firm had served in such dual capacities. In fact, I also at various times served as a trustee of charitable organizations while providing legal advice and assistance to them. And it is frequently done, even today, in the case of family members and relatives, where, for example, a person serves as a trustee or executor for parents, children, grandchildren, and other relatives, while also being their legal counsel. I knew of no policy of the Firm, nor any ethical or insurance-related prohibition against that. But, as long as Mr. Carr was mentally and otherwise competent, and as long as his brother John was alive, it was all a moot question anyway.

"Then, after the passage of years, favored brother John died in a tragic accident, and it was no longer a moot question. It was a real and immediate issue for me, because, on the one hand, I automatically stepped into the role of being the person responsible for Mr. Carr's care and for the handling of his financial affairs. More importantly, Mr. Carr's worst fears in earlier years became a part of the new reality when his estranged brother Jesse took advantage of Mr. Carr's vulnerable situation and got him to sign new documents, negating everything he had so carefully planned. By that time, he was 93 years old, had developed dementia, was functionally blind, was mostly immobile from arthritis, had serious congestive heart failure and was diabetic or prediabetic. Here was this long-time client, really brilliant in most of the time I worked with him, who had definite ideas about the disposition of his assets, and now all that he had worked and planned for was being canceled by family members who seemed to care only about his money.

"Now I am, and was, totally aware that the Carr family was a prominent and influential family, and I know it is not desirable to take on such community pillars in litigation. But I represented Alexander Carr, not the rest of the family, and he was in no position to help himself. He was a Carr, surely the most prominent of all the Carrs. He had counted on me and had extracted a vow from me that I would not let Jesse ever get in control of his financial affairs. I was the only one with any standing to protect him against this travesty.

"I thought about how to resolve this huge problem and did my best to resolve it in a quiet and low-key manner. I consulted with Rod Olson who, as all of you know, is a probate law specialist and someone who was familiar with the relevant factual background, having in fact drafted some of the more recent versions of Mr. Carr's estate planning documents. Our plan was to file a simple motion with the Probate Court requesting the

Court to advise as to whether I should honor the new and revised fiduciary documents which reversed 25 years of Mr. Carr's careful planning. I did not feel I could ignore and walk away from my commitments to secure justice, at least without first getting the oversight of the Court. Rod and I thought the Court would hold a hearing in a few weeks and rule on the matter. If the Court said the new Jesse-inspired documents should be honored, then I could walk away with a clear conscience that I had done what I could to protect him. I told the Probate Court that we simply wanted to lay out the facts for the Court's oversight and we would happily abide by whatever the Court decided. It is important for you to understand that I never asked the Court at that stage to uphold my status as his fiduciary; I just asked the Court to tell us what we should do because I could not ethically walk away from a possible abuse of a client I had sworn to protect, without at least raising a question so the Court could decide what needed to be done.

"Perhaps there were lawyers in the Firm, possibly some of you, who thought I was fighting to keep my position, which is not at all correct. It turned out the case was escalated by Jesse and his very aggressive lawyer who tried to make me the villain, saying I was tortiously interfering with a contract Mr. Carr had made, trying to hang on in order to get a big fee, being unfaithful to my fiduciary duties to Mr. Carr in not honoring his new documents. They filed a parallel lawsuit in the Circuit Court where they hoped to have a judge who was less sensitive to the vulnerability of older and ailing persons to signing any document put in front of them. They wanted a judge who would just presume Mr. Carr's competency to make wholesale changes in his long-standing estate plans. They thought they had succeeded in getting such a judge, and they expected they would win the race to judgment by getting a trial in the Circuit Court first, thus preempting the Probate Court's jurisdiction. The opposition sent a message to me addressed to Rod Olson, threatening me personally with financial ruin, as well as ruin to my personal and professional reputation if I did not give up. As you can imagine, I went through some troubled times, before deciding that my obligation to my client had to take priority over concerns about my own finances and reputation. So, I persevered.

"This Committee made me aware of its desire that the case be settled and that I should get out of it. I would have liked to have done that. Unfortunately, it takes two to settle a case, and at no time did the other side indicate a willingness to settle. In fact, we did not even have the option to walk away, without paying damages and attorney fees and, either directly or indirectly, admitting wrongdoing. I cannot convey to you the trauma I was suffering from this case. There were times when I wished I had never met or known Alexander Carr. But I have a passion for justice, and I put everything on the line in pursuit of that passion.

"I have been a lawyer and partner in this Firm for many years, and I have taken great pride in that association. I think I have brought much credit to the Firm through the years I have been here, while at the same time being the beneficiary of the Firm's support and counsel. But I am a lawyer, an individual lawyer with ethical and moral imperatives that also must be respected, in addition to being of member of this Firm. The Firm might have considered that, in its overall interest and the interest of all the lawyers in the firm, it would be better if the Carr case just disappeared, went away. I can understand those feelings, and I am sensitive to how my individual actions affect the Firm. But my desire to comply with the perspective and preferences of the Firm did not permit me to ignore my individual ethical responsibilities and commitments to a client who has paid us for legal protections against the very abuses to which he was now being subjected.

"I was much relieved with the results of this litigation, and I hoped that the Firm would also join in celebrating the victory of justice over predation which has been achieved in this remarkable trial. It will probably be the last trial in which I will have been involved, and of all the difficult and challenging trials I have had, this one will be recorded in my memory as the hardest and most traumatic, and yet possibly the finest of them all. If I were called upon to choose a high note for my exit from the Firm, this is the one I would choose, with great pride.

"Some of you might have concerns about whether this litigation, notwithstanding the favorable outcome for justice and the rule of law, has fractured the firm's relationship with the Carr family. I am happy to be able to tell you it has not. The brother Jesse lies terminally ill at this moment, with possibly only days to live. Every single one of the Carr heirs – Alexander's four children – have come over to our side as this matter and the trial developed, and I think I now have a very good relationship with all of them, including Rand, who during part of the time was backing Jesse's efforts. Mr. Carr, to the extent he can express himself, seems very happy, and his household staff has exhibited nothing but cooperation and respect. So, if there is concern about possible friction with the Carr family in the future, I think those concerns can be put aside.

"I cannot speak to the requirements of our malpractice insurance carrier that is apparently not comfortable with my role as a fiduciary as well as an attorney. I can understand the theoretical concerns, but of course those concerns are resolved and behind us in this case. Yet I understand that insurance companies tend to make decisions on a statistical basis for the entire population, without delving into the facts of specific situations. In any event, I do not challenge its decision, if there indeed has been such a decision, to require me to separate from the Firm if I continue as a fiduciary for Mr. Carr.

"The fact is, I have had a fabulous career. I have had a complement of what must be as fascinating and meaningful experiences as is possible for a lawyer to have. I am financially secure, so I have no concerns in that respect. I will be able to minister to Mr. Carr for the rest of his life and then work with his children when he passes, and that will be yet another fine experience to have. I will be able to devote more time to my family and friends, and I might even take time to write my memoirs, or other writings based on some of my experiences, that I would never have the time to do if I continued here as a full-time lawyer. I've always wanted to be a writer. So, it is a blessing that I must go. I will miss being here. Inertia is such a force in our lives that we tend to stick with what we know, and in what we feel secure. But security and familiarity are not the only virtues. There is a world out there I still want to discover and embrace, for whatever time I am allotted. I just recommend to each of you that you keep your focus on the important things and learn to recognize and distinguish them from the things that are temporal and passing.

"I must say that, although I and my family will not be significantly impacted financially as a result of my departure, I frankly do not think the departing compensation that has been offered to me is a proper and fitting way to acknowledge my contributions and the commitment to fidelity to which I have adhered, that has motivated me and has resulted in an extraordinary victory for justice. I believe the Firm would honor itself if it took another look at that remaining bit of stain that mars our relationship, which I wish could continue to be constructive and positive.

"Farewell, and may justice be ever the light of your path, as I am sure it will be. I would like to remain for a short while, like a couple of weeks, while I get my things in order, say good-bye to some friends, and that sort of thing. In the meanwhile, I wish you only the best."

"Wow!" said one of the members. "I can see now why you have won so many big cases. That was amazing!" Carl Heimat hastened, almost ran, from the far end of the table to shake Ted's hand and say how much he admired Ted and thanked him for coming. Others followed, but the member who had interviewed him, Adam Ford, had joined the meeting by remote conference telephone and said nothing. Ted had a final handshake with the Chairman, who said, "Of course you can take your time leaving. And the Committee will be back in touch with you shortly."

A couple of days later, the Chairman came by to see him and said, "As I think you probably sensed, the Executive Committee was very impressed with what you had to say and the way in which you comported yourself. I don't think either of us should try to rethink your decision to leave, but we have decided to give you a much-increased bonus for your achievements at the Firm this year and through the years. Thank you."

Ted responded, "I am glad that there will still remain a good and positive relationship between the Firm and me. I will still be retaining Rod Olson for legal matters relating to Mr. Carr, and there will likely be other legal matters that will cause me to revisit this former home of mine. I wish you only the best, and I thank you for hearing me out and for giving me a 'thank you' going-away bonus. It is appreciated."

"Would you like the Firm to give you a going-away dinner or reception?" asked the Chairman.

Ted immediately replied, "Absolutely not. It would be awkward for everyone. I think it best that I just fade away, like an old soldier."

The conversation was at an end. The lawyers shook hands, and the deal was done.

CHAPTER TWENTY-TWO

REFLECTIONS

After the EC Chairman left Ted's office and closed the door, Ted sat in his swivel chair and looked out his window, trying to grasp the reality of what had just happened. He *really* would be leaving the Firm, in many ways his home, where he had surely spent more waking hours in the last nearly half a century than in his own home. Leaving! If he should ever set foot in the Firm in the future, how would it feel – more like a happy reunion with friends, or as a stranger waiting in the reception room? The Firm would surely change. New faces would come in; old faces would exit, one way or another. Is it possible that at some future point he would come back to the Firm on a visit and nobody would even know who he was?

Well, the jolt of the change would surely be softened for a while by the fact that he would still be retaining Rod Olson as counsel on all the Carr legal matters, but he knew this would largely be handled by telephone and electronic communications, rarely requiring in-person visits. And how would he feel about seeing his former partners at bar association meetings or restaurants, or anywhere? Would it be the same? Then a special regret came to mind: He would no longer be getting the interoffice mail notices telling of anniversaries, milestones, victories, marriages, new babies – all the personal news that made the Firm seem so much like a big family. Leaving was more than just leaving. It would be a terminal thing, attenuating gradually from full engagement to nothingness.

He thought about himself. Who is Ted Born, after all? His own personal identity was so interwoven with the Firm that, when he thought of himself or identified himself to others, it would be: "I'm Ted Born, I'm a partner at - ." Ted knew he would always keep his identity as a lawyer, because he knew there was no doubt he would continue to keep up his law license, and he would continue selectively to handle cases for clients. But it would be so different. Not only had he habitually associated himself with the Firm, but many other lawyers had told him that when his Firm was mentioned, Ted's name was what came to mind. It would not only be different, but strange and unnatural. He would have a little time before he made his last trip out the door, a little time to get used to a new phase of his life. There would surely be joy and opportunities in the new world, but the old world was important, too, a part of his experiences, his memories, and a large part of who he had become.

Ted looked around the room at all the wall hangings – a painting, a few photographs, a lot of certificates and plaques: ODK, Raven Society, Law Review, Order of the Coif and diplomas from his collegiate days; Bar Association and Court Admission certificates; a "Best Lawyers in America" certification; an American Law Institute certificate; a surprise appreciation plaque given by his law school students; commendations from the Association for Retarded Citizens for pro bono legal work that had resulted in important new rights for them, and a host of other plaques and certificates. Others remained stuffed away in storage, because there was no room for them on his walls. In looking at the memorabilia, Born was somewhat embarrassed that his wall hangings had seemed so self-congratulatory, but they had served the practical purpose of reassuring clients that they were dealing with a competent lawyer. "I'm just an ordinary person, just happen to be a lawyer blessed - did I say 'blessed'? – with some extraordinary experiences, nothing more," Born told himself, checking the sin of false pride. Besides, as much as Born knew that these "accolades" – as Jason Smith had called them – were just community thank-you notes that would eventually find their way into a landfill somewhere and had little intrinsic value, for Ted they were still markers of memorable events in his life, mostly associated with his life as a lawyer. The memories were important to him, if to no one else, because they were *his* memories. Subsequent generations would have to consign them to oblivion; Ted could no more part with them than with the occasions they brought to mind, etched on the continuing wall of his life events.

Ted began thinking of the practical things that would confront him, like what to do with his over-sized desk and his office furniture. He could probably use a couple of wing-backed chairs in his home, with new fabric coverings, but he already had a satisfactory desk at home and would not need this one.

Moreover, what would he do with his clients and his files? He had no intention of trying to hang onto any particular clients, although he had close personal relationships with most of them. They would know to call him if they had future needs, and he might try to help them, if appropriate. But he already knew he would not want actively to seek any new work, and he would be happy if they transferred their future work to others who were remaining in the Firm. But he had in mind writing his memoirs and would need copies of some documents from archival files. All this would lie ahead of him, to deal with in the next couple of weeks. For now, he just wanted to leave the office to sort things out, and go home, where he could see and talk with Lydia, in serenity.

Lydia greeted him with a smile and a hug. "You are home early, unheard of! How did it go today, Ted?"

"It was a different kind of day. As we have known it would happen for the last few weeks, it happened today. I have officially resigned from the Firm, and I am no longer a partner there anymore. I will have some time to clear out, but it looks like you are going to have to put up with me here at the house more than you ever have before. It's good we added on that addition to the house to provide a study for me, because I am going to need it more than ever," Ted said in a subdued and thoughtful tone.

Lydia looked both sympathetic and sad: "I can't imagine what it will be like. Ever since we met, you have been with the Firm, first as an associate and then as a partner. The Firm has been the backdrop of our whole marriage, our whole life together. I feel like we are married to the Firm, and divorce has always been one of those unthinkable things about our relationship to each other, and to the Firm. How is it going to work?"

"I will of course continue to be Mr. Carr's power of attorney holder and his Trustee, and that will occupy a lot of my time, and I will be well compensated for it. I will be working with Rod Olson at the Firm on all the Carr legal matters, so I will at least have that contact, and there will be other occasions when I will be involved in some ongoing matters. I will also continue to take on some other work on the side. But I want to phase out all the legal work gradually, because we are financially secure, and this gives us an opportunity to enter a new and potentially wonderful phase of our lives. We need to look at it as something whose time has come. I am 72 years old, and most people my age retired years earlier, and even with this move, I'm not really retiring; I'll still be working. I guess that a not-so-welcome side issue in this situation is that I will be home for lunch most days, which I don't want to be a burden for you. I will do what I can to make it easier - we can eat out more often, or bring in take-out food, or something," Ted offered.

"Oh, don't worry about that, Ted. I have to make my own lunch most days and it's hardly any more trouble to do two lunches than one. I love you, and I will be just so glad to see more of you. It's really nice that we like each other!" Lydia reassured him.

"Not just 'like'," Ted said, "but 'LOVE'! If it had not been real love between us, I don't know how you would have put up with my awful work hours and habits all these years. The law really is a jealous mistress, and you have been shortchanged at times, but I'm going to try to make it up to you, at least a little bit, during the rest of our lives. It is kind of exciting to think: We can take long trips together; we can spend a lot more time at our house in Maine in the summers; and we can sleep a little later in the morning and have an unbelievable amount of flexibility in our schedules, maybe even get some af-ternoon naps!"

"You make it sound wonderful, but we've been mar-ried a long time, and I know you well enough to know that you will always be busy with projects of some kind. You will take on the Presidency of some more civic organizations - if there are any you haven't already headed. And you will have lots to do. By the same token, I've taken on a lot of commitments in my schedule, with the regular choir at Church, also the handbell choir, the civic chorus that gives performances at nursing homes, and we have house plants that need to be watered – and a small dog. These may sound mundane, but they are real. It won't be as easy as it seems, but somehow we'll find a way, we'll manage," Lydia said.

"Well, I do want to write my memoirs," Ted interjected. I've had an interesting life, and you've had an interesting life, and together we've shared so, so much in joy and sometimes sorrow. Writing about it ought to help us get our arms around what it all means, Lydia. Isn't that the only question that matters: What does it all mean? I think we can come up with some worthwhile thoughts that might resonate with other people. There are not many things we haven't had to face, and deal with, in our lives. We have a lot to say."

Lydia sighed, "But would anyone want to listen? Young people think they are immortal and will live forever, retaining all their youthful vigor for the duration, neither needing nor interested in our thoughts or counsel. Older people, on the other hand, may come to realize the wisdom of experience, but at their age it does them little good. Such is life."

"I'm sure it is going to take us some time to adjust, though. We need to let Rebecca know. She would not want to learn this from someone other than her Dad. We can call her in Charleston tomorrow. At this point, we could start getting acquainted with those afternoon naps, and more acquainted with each other," Ted added, as he put his arms around Lydia.

CHAPTER TWENTY-THREE

A VISIT FROM DAVE THOMPSON

One of the first of Ted's partners to come to talk with Ted about his departure was Dave Thompson. Ted and Dave had tried a classic case together some fifteen years earlier, the case they referred to as the "mock orange" case, when Dave was a new young associate. They had not tried many cases together since that time as Thompson became a general litigator and Ted had been occupied more with setting up the Firm's premier intellectual property group of lawyers and trying IP and antitrust cases. Still, they had developed a bond from that trial that was strong and enduring, with mutual respect. Dave Thompson was African American, and Ted was Caucasian, but, as Ted often pointed out, our ancestors all came from Africa at one time or another, and we are all human and all brothers and sisters.

Thompson came into Ted's office and said, "I've just heard a nasty rumor, Ted. I heard you are leaving the Firm. Say it ain't so, Ted!"

"Dave, you are one of the ones on my list to make a special visit with, before I leave. We've been through the fiery furnace together and lived to tell about it, and we bonded. You are very special to me. But, yes, it is true. I'm leaving. I don't like the idea, but it looks like that's the only way, and maybe it's time to leave anyway. I had the option to stay, but I would have had to renounce everything I had accomplished for my client, with great personal trauma, and I would have had to go back on a commitment to that client, who trusted me and was depending on me. I couldn't do that. They - the Executive Committee - tell me that our malpractice insurance carrier will not allow me to serve as a Trustee for my client Alexander Carr and simultaneously serve as his legal counsel and power of attorney holder - too much potential for conflict of interest and intra-family squabbles, I gather is the thinking. But I committed, in fact, made a vow to him, that I would protect him and his finances from the grasp of his estranged brother, and he wanted me in place, after his first choice of a favorite brother, to carry out that commitment. We have just finished a lengthy God-awful litigation where I was personally sued and had my name vilified, just for trying to do as he directed me.

We won, even though the odds at times seemed heavily against us – about the same odds as we had in our mock orange trial! And after winning and being vindicated – both ourselves and the client - in that terrible litigation, I could not just walk away from it and abandon my role as his trustee and attorney-in-fact. He has dementia, you see, and he needs protection. I really had no choice. As you know, I am passionate about justice."

"Sounds to me like a way could have been found for you to stay. Do you feel the Firm let you down?" Dave asked.

"I don't think that way, Dave," Ted replied. "I don't allow myself to ask that question. I tell myself this could be a blessing, something I ought to do anyway. Maybe I just needed to be prompted. It is not as though I don't have other options. Even at my age, if I wanted to, I'm sure I could go to another firm and continue. It's not that THIS Firm let me down. It's more that the whole universe of law firms has gone off in a direction that is different from my concept of what the profession of law is all about. I wouldn't want to swap one incompatible for another. Law firms have become so – how do I say it – *corporate*. It's big business, and I still cling to the vision of the law as a profession, where one lawyer has a relationship with one client, multiplied many times over, of course. But the relationship is, or ought to be, a highly personal one, with a sense of commitment and trust on both sides. That was the way it was with Mr. Carr and me. And the Firm was looking at it in terms of, 'let's not get into messy litigation, especially when there are prominent people on the other side, it's not good PR, not good for our corporate interests.' Now, I grant you that public relations considerations are legitimate to factor in. But, once you have committed to represent a client, a lawyer's duty is to see it through, regardless any negative PR for oneself. I am in many ways an old-fashioned lawyer, I know, but there are times when the duty of being a professional – as an individual lawyer with moral and ethical values - has to trump other considerations. I feel I was right to take the stand I took, and I was vindicated, and a just result was achieved for a trusting client. That did not seem to make any difference to some of our lawyers. As much as I have always loved this Firm and have taken pride in being a part of it, it's not a good fit for me anymore. Possibly I bear a lot of the responsibility for the misfit, but I am a lawyer with personal as well as corporate responsibilities, and I cannot ignore conscience."

"Do you think those of us who remain here have sold out, have accommodated ourselves to a system that is devoid of personal and passionate commitment?" asked Dave.

"No, not at all, Dave. A person could practice here for years and years and never have a situation like I had. You likely can be a fine and conscientious lawyer practically all of the time, just as I have tried to be, and never encounter a dilemma that pits your conscience against the general corporate mentality that often hovers in the background, out of sight. You are a fine and conscience-driven lawyer yourself. The odds are high that you will have no problems that test your allegiances. I hope you will stick with the Firm, Dave. The Firm needs you and is so much better because you are here. I really am not bad-mouthing the Firm. I am just regretting the trends in the practice of law. But, despite those trends, the law is still a noble profession, an opportunity to pursue and promote justice. Other than the Church, and its moral teachings, the law is all we really have that holds society and civilization together, even when it is imperfect," Ted answered.

"Ever since our mock orange trial, I have been turning over in my mind, 'What is justice?' I haven't quite got it figured out," Dave said.

"We're still working on that, I guess, and I don't have the delineations fine-tuned, either. It's a work in progress, and probably always will be. For most of us, we're trying to get there, and sometimes we seem to make progress, and sometimes we go in the other direction. Our lawmakers make mistakes, like all the rest of us - sometimes for lack of information or good judgment, sometimes because of political pressure from particular groups, or even their own self-interest. The same for our judges. It's complicated, too, because there is always this balancing of what is good and right for the country as a whole, or the community as a whole, and the general wisdom from all that balancing effort often turns out to be not quite right in individual cases. As a society, I think we generally have good intentions, goodwill, and we are searching for the New Jerusalem, even when it seems out of reach. We lawyers are critical to this process, because we actually think about justice as the central core of our profession, and our actions in the courtrooms probably contribute more to our goal of justice than anything else in society. Why? Because we have the opportunity to make judges and jurors focus on what is 'justice' in concrete fact-based settings where individual litigants are heard from in real, not hypothetical, cases. The composite results of those efforts advance us closer to achieving real justice than anything else that impacts the cause. For that reason, lawyers are the great hope of humanity, and give hope for progress in the search for justice. Keep the faith, Dave!" Ted reflected.

"Ted, I often think back to our mock orange case. We had some people who had been killed or badly injured in an automobile accident case, mainly through no fault of their own. A tire blew out, and the people in the borrowed car didn't realize the tire was bad - can't really fault them - and they sued the tire company for compensation. We defended on the basis that the accident wasn't our fault, that the tire was so worn out it shouldn't have been on the public roads in the first place. Our client had made a good tire that had given good service, longer than you would have expected of that tire, and the tire had been abused. So, the accident wasn't our fault, and yet it also wasn't the fault of the little girl who lost her life, or the others who were badly injured. So, in a way, it wasn't the 'fault' of anyone involved in the accident. If it was anyone's fault, it was the fault of the man that loaned them the vehicle. And yet it was Bess who wanted to borrow the van, and her uncle Sam Johnson was nice enough to lend it to her. He made no charge to them for their use of his van, and probably he might not have realized the bad condition of the tire. He was trying to be nice, do a favor. Yes, I know, he should have checked the tires before lending the van, and I guess his niece Bess should have checked them also, before getting in and driving the van, but most people in real-world circumstances would have just assumed they were all right, especially for just a short trip. After all, when you borrow a car, are you expected to examine *everything*, not just the tires?

"So, we have death, injuries, and bereavement, and no one gets compensated," Dave continued, "because our company, the tire maker, was not at fault. What is justice in a case like that? And, yes, I know there was attempted bribery by our opposition, and I know we were fortunate to get a fair jury that ruled in our favor, and I know there was some exploitation motive by greedy lawyers on the other side. But even though I was satisfied at the time that the verdict was just, I find myself being troubled about it. I know it's not fair for a manufacturer to have to continue to be responsible for damage occurring on account of a product that had outlived its safeness and usefulness, because otherwise you turn them into insurance companies for inevitable accidents, and you reduce the incentives for people to assume personal responsibility for proper maintenance, but I keep having flashbacks, wondering if there wasn't something missing in our system of justice in that case. I can't get the photograph of the beautiful little lifeless girl out of my mind. Does any of that bother you?" asked Dave.

"Certainly, it does, and it did at the time," Ted answered. "I had tremendous compassion for the plaintiffs, especially the children who died or were injured. And you and I expressed that compassion in a personal way. But we were lawyers and advocates making fair and correct arguments about the law, as was our obligation to our clients. We were neither judge nor jury. We put on the evidence and made our arguments, and the jury agreed with us, even though their sympathy must have been with the injured and dead. We fulfilled our role in the system of justice, just as we were supposed to do. We had our obligation to our clients. That is what lawyers do, and it is what we must always do. You can wonder about the results in a particular case, but when you have been a lawyer faithful to your client, to whom you owe your uncompromised loyalty, that helps make our system work. There is still that question we need to ask: 'Does justice require that there be a legal remedy for every injury, disease or bad situation that is not the fault of anyone?' I tend to doubt it. A child tragically drowns in the undertow on a beach excursion, perhaps using a surfboard. Should the surfboard manufacturer be liable? What about a lot of forms of cancer and other diseases, where we cannot pinpoint a cause or show that it was the fault of somebody else? Life involves certain things that happen, from a child's skinned knee to death from old age, that are not the fault of someone else's bad acts. It is sad, but there are no guarantees of tomorrow or of what tomorrow might bring for any of us. Lawsuits are for compensating others for unnecessary harm caused by a defendant who has done something wrong; when bad things happen, it does not necessarily imply that a lawsuit is the answer. A part of life is that all of us teeter on the brink of extinguishment every day, not always because of the fault of someone else. Still, we savor the joy of each day we live, and we have compassion regardless of fault. I think justice was done in our case, in very, very difficult circumstances for our side."

"I can't disagree with you, Ted. I just want you to know how much I hate to see you go. I wish there was another way. You think about things. You have a conscience and compassion. You set an example for the rest of us."

"Dave, *you* have set a great example for all of us, too. I have grown so much in mind and conscience from knowing you and, as I so often say, bonding with you. The Firm is so fortunate to have you. Every blessing I hope for you.," Ted said.

The two shook hands in a moment when time seemed to stand still, looking each other in the eye. "Remember the 'brotherhood of suffering.'" Dave said. "I haven't forgotten, Dave," said Ted. "We are both alumni of that fraternity. Somehow, we summoned up hope and kept struggling, and then we saw a rainbow's end in the distance, a rewarding destination called the 'brotherhood of joy.' There's merit in remembering both, but the joy, and the expectation of joy, is special. That's why we endure the suffering." Dave nodded, smiled, then turned to go, and closed the door behind him, with a final glance backward.

Others came to say goodbyes and good wishes in the days that followed, while Ted Born packed up and prepared to make a final exit. He sold his large desk to the Firm, wondering but not asking who would be sitting behind that desk, meeting the challenges that would inevitably come, listening to clients sitting across that desk relating their dilemmas and hoping for answers. Born canceled his contract for space in the parking deck, packed up the last of his belonging, got in his car, went through the exit gate, looked back at his once office building, and moved on.

CHAPTER TWENTY-FOUR

JESSE AND THE CLIENT

Jason Smith first called Ted Born with the news. "Ted, I wanted you to know that Jesse Carr just passed away. He had prostate cancer that had metastasized. He did not want anyone to know his medical situation. That's why I had not clued you in earlier. Makes you wonder, though, what if he had won the case? What would have happened next? Rand, I guess, might have taken over. Jesse's wife Candace is beside herself. Don't know about funeral arrangements yet."

"Thanks for calling, Jason," said Ted. "I am genuinely sorry to hear of his passing, although I knew he was ill and had gotten hints that his illness was very serious. You know, I was wondering, after we won the case, whether I would be encountering him at Mr. Carr's house when he would presumably be coming to visit him. I was wondering whether there would be awkwardness, perhaps bitterness on Jesse's part. I wondered if it would be possible for us to have a good conversation so I could assure him I bore him no ill will and was doing my best to be responsive to Mr. Carr's needs. I really had hoped we could establish a good relationship, going forward. And now, that's an impossibility. He's gone, without any reconciliation. I regret his passing, and my regret is compounded by knowing there was no reconciliation before his passing. I really had wanted to wipe the past off my screen and let him know I truly forgave him and harbored no ill will. I'm really sorry. Let me know if I can do anything."

Other family members called Ted also, to report on Jesse's passing. Finally, Ted got an unexpected call from Jesse's widow Candace. "Mr. Born, I don't know if you have heard that Jesse has passed away. I am so upset. I have to make funeral arrangements, and I don't know what to do. I know you have control of Zander's funds, and I wondered if you could give me enough money to cover his funeral expenses so he can have a decent funeral."

Born responded, "Mrs. Carr, I want to do what I can to help. First, I will need to get the consent of all the children, because there is no authorization in the Trust to make a substantial payment like that from Zander's funds, and of course Zander himself has been ruled incapacitated to give such consent. But his children are the residuary beneficiaries under the will of Mr. Carr, and if they all consent, then I feel comfortable doing it, because it will one day be their money. Let me contact them and see what they say, and I will be back in touch with you. I know you need an answer right away. I am genuinely sorry about your husband's passing, and I just regret we never had a chance to get reconciled with each other, but I wanted you to know I bore him no ill will, whatsoever."

Ted called the Carr heirs and pointed out to them that, because Jesse had preceded Zander Carr in death, the modest inheritance he might otherwise have received from Zander would lapse, and that the amount Candace had requested was less than his inheritance would have been. They all agreed Ted should provide the funds, which were fairly substantial. Ted wrote a check for the requested amount, bought a condolence card, put it and the check in an envelope, and took it to the home of Candace. He rang the doorbell, and Candace came to the door. There seemed to be voices in the background, presumably from others coming to comfort Candace, but Ted did not see them and did not attempt to enter the house. "Mrs. Carr, here is a condolence note, and there is a check enclosed for the amount you requested. I want you to know that I and all of Zander's children are very saddened by Jesse's passing. I wish I could have gotten to know him better."

"Thank you, Mr. Born. We will have the service at the church day after tomorrow, and I hope you can be there," Candace said. Ted assured her he would be there. Ted had approached this in-person meeting with Candace with some concern as to how it would go, considering Candace's rather loud and open hostility at the trial, but in this moment of sorrow, rancor had no play. He wondered if he would see Candace on some future occasion at Mr. Carr's house, perhaps on a friendly social visit to see her brother-in-law. Perhaps they could make amends under those circumstances. Then he remembered that Mr. Carr and Candace got along with each other even more poorly than Mr. Carr and Jesse. He guessed he probably wouldn't be seeing her again, unless it might be an accidental encounter in a grocery store or some incidental place like that. Indeed, to Ted's knowledge, Candace never paid a visit to Mr. Carr after Jesse's death.

Born attended Jesse's funeral service, which happened to be at the same Church Born belonged to. He sat near the back of the Church during the service, trying to be as inconspicuous as possible. There were no personal remembrances from friends, as sometimes occurred in such services. The homily was rather general and followed the usual liturgy. Jesse had transferred his membership to the Church only a year or two earlier, apparently because it was more conveniently located to his home than his former downtown Church. As the Minister referred to various meetings he had had with Jesse after Jesse joined the Church, Ted wondered if Jesse had discussed the recent litigation or had made comments about him, Ted, in the course of any of the sessions with the clergy. If so, no one in the Church had ever mentioned it to Ted, and Ted hoped his personal reputation within the Church would have been a sufficient rebuttal to any negative comments Jesse might have made. In any case, it was all over now. Ted quickly and silently left the service at the conclusion, without encountering any family members, but having signed the register of attendees. Ted noted that Mr. Carr was in attendance in a wheelchair, as Earl Robbins had promised he would handle. There was a separate private burial at the Carr cemetery space, space which Mr. Carr had purchased for all Carr family members who wished to be buried there, but Ted respected the private family-only character of the burial and did not attend that event.

Ted had developed a close friendship with Mr. Carr's butler/chauffeur Earl Robbins and got nearly daily reports from him about Mr. Carr, supplementing his frequent personal visits, and he likewise got fairly frequent inquiries from Mr. Robbins about any and all matters relating to the household. Robbins had taken Mr. Carr to Jesse's funeral, but remarked to Ted that he was not sure Mr. Carr really took in what was going on. Ted went to see Mr. Carr the day after the funeral and said, "Mr. Carr, that was a nice service for Jesse."

"Did you say 'Jesse'? What about him?" he asked.

"His funeral. You know, you were there," Ted answered.

"What happened to Jesse?" he asked.

"He passed away, Mr. Carr, it was very sad," Ted replied.

"What happened to him? Why didn't anybody tell me?" he asked. Mr. Robbins, who was standing in the door, just shook his head.

"I understand he had cancer. His funeral was yesterday. Do you remember?" Born asked.

"I knew nothing about it. Are you sure? Jesse was supposed to come over." He frowned and looked very perplexed.

"Mr. Carr, it's all right. Jesse is not in pain anymore. Let's talk about something else I wanted to tell you. You know, you and I have worked together for a long time, more than 25 years. You were a client first, and then a friend, and you have always had my admiration. I don't know if you will remember all the things that have happened in the last few years, and I won't try to recount them, but I wanted to remind you that I once made a vow to you, a solemn vow, that if anything happened to your brother John, that I would step in and see that you were taken care of, and that your finances would be secure. I wanted you to know that I have kept my vow. It wasn't easy. I had to leave my law firm, but here I am. I have no regrets, and I would do it all again. I am still in the process of fulfilling that vow, as my responsibilities under it are continuing. I am going to see that you get the best of everything that you need. I am here for you, and Mr.

Robbins knows to call me if you need anything and if there is anything I can do," Ted said.

"I'm glad you are here. I'm glad. I've had a good life. Thank you," Mr. Carr said.

"Yes, the important thing is, I am here for you. You have someone who will take up for you and take care of you. Ted said.

"Is lunch ready?" he asked.

"Not quite time for it, Mr. Carr. But it will be here in a little while. Mr. Robbins and the lady that does your meals will take care of that," Ted assured him.

Ted said his good-bye and walked out the door with Mr. Robbins. "He's going downhill pretty fast, isn't he?" Ted commented.

"You know, Mr. Born, he has some good days and some bad days. Some days he can remember some things, 'specially things that happened a long time ago. But he has trouble with recent things, though sometimes that's better, too. I think the shock of Mr. Jesse's death and funeral really confused him bad, and he don't remember he even went to the funeral, or that there was a funeral," Robbins said.

"Well, we just have to accept the circumstances and move on. Some things are beyond what anyone can do. Doesn't he have a doctor's appointment coming up soon?" Ted asked.

"Day after tomorrow. Not sure it will do much good, nothing much the doctor can do, says he's just in decline, nothing specific like cancer, but his body is just wearing out, and of course, his memory is going. But we will be there. The Doc might adjust his medication, and maybe that will help. Just between us, I really need a hip replacement myself, but I don't want to take the time off to get it because he needs me here right now," Robbins said.

"We'll see if we can work that out, Earl - I hope it's OK for me to call you 'Earl,' and you can certainly call me 'Ted'." Robbins looked relieved, "I appreciate that. These formalities get in the way," he said.

Ted left and was thinking of two things he needed to do. He needed to get Mr. Robbins some time off to get his hip replacement done, and the sooner, the better, as Mr. Carr would be needing him increasingly as time went on. The second thing is that he needed to be thinking ahead for the day when Mr. Carr would pass away, starting with picking out the casket and vault, writing the obituary and pre-paying the funeral expenses. The estate would get a discount for prepayment, which is what Mr. Carr would have wanted, and all the details would be in place to help the Carr survivors.

CHAPTER TWENTY-FIVE

THE LAST DAYS

Mr. Carr had his doctor's appointment, and Ted Born made it a point to be there, as he wanted to speak personally to the doctor after the appointment. The doctor first apologized for having supported the position that Mr. Carr was competent to sign the power of attorney favoring Jesse. "At the time, I really let myself get influenced by my general strong preference for family, frankly, to provide the caregiving for a person like Mr. Carr. But now that I've read the Judge's opinion, I can see how wrong I was in this case, and the fact you have come to see me validates his choice of you. I apologize," confessed Dr. Hargrove.

"No apologies necessary, Doctor. I didn't come for or expect apologies. We all have to make judgments at times that are not based on full and accurate information, and we do the best we can. What is your assessment of his condition now?" Ted asked.

"Well, its tenuous. He's 95 or 96 years old. He is functionally blind. He has congestive heart failure, which he could live with for a while, but it could take him out just any day. We have been saying he was pre-diabetic, but it's looking like he has crossed, or is about to cross the point where it is looking like full-blown diabetes. He does like rich ice cream, and he is running a danger of his blood glucose being too high or suddenly dropping too low, so controlling it is going to be increasingly an issue, probably have to go to shots, and someone will have to give him the shots and monitor his glucose. He has a bad back and general arthritis problems and has difficulty walking. To top it all, he is a definite fall risk – he's already fallen a few times, fortunately without bone breakage thus far - but his bones are brittle, and he could be totally immobilized any time he has another bad fall. And, as you know, the dementia is accelerating pretty fast, perhaps in part because he cannot see well enough to read the newspaper or to engage normally with other people. There is not much I can do to prevent his general decline, just needs to keep taking the medication I've already prescribed, try to prevent any more falls, be sure he always has sitters around the clock – maybe two sitters, because one sitter might not be able to handle situations that could come up. As I mentioned, if we determine he has to start taking insulin, someone will have to give it who knows how to do it. I don't think we absolutely have to do it right yet, but soon, if he lasts much longer," Dr. Hargrove advised.

"Dr. Hargrove, Mr. Carr endowed a Chair in your honor at the University Medical Center, didn't he?" Born asked.

"He did, indeed, and he has always been very special to me because of that, and also just because we have had a long and good physician-patient relationship," the Doctor answered.

"You can be assured I will do everything possible to keep him safe and comfortable, and I will try to think of ways to stimulate his mind, although I can't think just how right now," Born said.

"In my experience, one of the most important things is to avoid falls. When a patient in his situation has a bad fall, that is generally the beginning of the end," the Doctor observed.

Ted thanked the Doctor and left. Earl Robbins had already left with Mr. Carr. Ted determined he would double-up on the sitters for Mr. Carr, and that would also allow Earl Robbins to get his hip replacement surgery done, helped by the presence of the additional sitters to care for Mr. Carr in his absence.

Robbins got his hip replacement and surprisingly was back on the job within two weeks, able to climb stairs

- slowly at first - and do most of his normal responsibilities. The extra set of sitters really helped, even when Robbins returned, as Mr. Carr began to need two persons to help him get from one place to another within his house. He was spending more of his time in bed, not often getting to the sitting room where he had been spending so much time not so long before. Once, he had what seemed to be a heart attack, as he cried out in pain. Ted Born was called in the middle of the night, and he in turn called the paramedics to take Mr. Carr to the hospital, where he went to meet them, after dressing quickly. It happened that Dr. Hargrove was out of town at the time, and his backup came to the hospital to check on Mr. Carr. It seemed to have been a mini-stroke, and he was sent home after a couple of days in the hospital. When Dr. Hargrove returned, he told Ted that, had he been available, he would not have approved sending him to the hospital, where he would have to go through that "meat grinder," as the Doctor called it. "He is ready to die, Ted, and the kindest thing is to let him die at home," he advised. Ted was troubled by the assessment, as he was naturally conditioned to solving problems and making things - and people - better. It seemed cold and cruel, and he, as Mr. Carr's primary responsible caretaker, did not believe he could have responsibly made any choice other than sending Mr. Carr to the hospital.

But there would not be another occasion for Ted to have to make a choice about home or hospital. After a time, Mr. Carr's breathing became labored, and hospice

was called in. He rallied briefly, and the hospice people took a break for a few days. During that break, the
breathing became increasingly labored. Ted spent an
afternoon with him and said, "Mr. Carr, this is Ted Born.
I wanted you to know that I am here *with* you, here *for*
you. How do you feel?" At first there was no response.
Then, amid labored deep breathing, Mr. Carr uttered, "A
good life. Time to go, time to move on. It's beautiful."
There was a faint smile on his face. His emaciated hand
moved to touch Ted's hand, with more firmness than Ted
expected, then fell back.

A few days later, Ted was called again, in the night,
and this time he called hospice and Dr. Hargrove, and
then the Carr heirs, and finally the funeral home. Mr.
Carr was at peace. His struggles were at an end, but Ted
took consolation in that last conversation, that Mr. Carr
was ready to move on, and that he smiled and seemed to
visualize something he called "beautiful." He thought
back to Dr. Hargrove's advice that his client and friend
was ready to go. Ted thought, how hard it is to imagine
that people really get to the point where they are actually
ready to move on, especially hard to imagine when we
are younger and healthier. It was also comforting that
Mr. Carr in his last breaths, did not seem to think of it
as the end. Maybe it's like leaving a law firm, the end of
one life, but the beginning of another life that could be
beautiful. In a way, he could relate to Mr. Carr's passing.

The obituary had long been written, with a glowing account of Mr. Carr's laurels and warm references to his remarkable life and philanthropy. His dark suit and red tie were ready, and the casket was, if not red, at least rosewood. At the Church, a bagpiper played on the sidewalk in front as friends arrived to pay their respects. Then the service began with the bagpiper entering the Church playing "Highland Cathedral," and as he approached the chancel, the organ broke in with its own lofty chords of "Highland Cathedral," resonating harmoniously with the bagpiper, who then retreated slowly down the nave of the Church until the notes faded when he reached the outside and piped off into the distance. The service appropriately called to mind Mr. Carr's generosity and service and the multifaceted legacy he had bequeathed to community and family.

A reception/visitation was held in the Church parlor, attended by many whose paths had crossed Mr. Carr's. Ted spoke to Earl Robbins at the reception, "Earl, I know you must be wondering about your own future, after having been with Mr. Carr now for more than 30 years. I can only say he still needs you, and I need you, as we deal with the house and his possessions. Of course, you are also in his will, as I am sure you know, and I will be distributing that to you just as soon as I can. We won't be needing any of the other staff, but they will get severance pay, pretty generous pay, I think. But I hope you can stay for a while, maybe a year or more, as we deal with things. Can you do that?"

"I sure am glad to hear you say that. It's not easy getting a new job at my age. If I have enough time, I think I can find some other work, but it's good to know I don't have to go out and start looking tomorrow," Earl replied.

"I'll be at the house tomorrow, and we'll get started. See you then, and blessings." Ted said.

CHAPTER TWENTY-SIX

SETTLING

Ted Born drove to the house again that used to be Mr. Carr's home. Now, it was in a state of limbo. Ted was in charge of liquidating and settling the estate, but no one was really the "owner" of the house anymore. In time, the Will would have to be probated. However, there was cash in the Trust, and that would be available for expenses while the probate process played out. He hoped the beneficiaries would all be cooperative and sign consents that would eliminate the necessity of advertising and incurring avoidable delays. Indeed, it turned out they were all totally cooperative.

Ted looked around the house, completely empty except for Earl Robbins. There were some major tasks that needed to be undertaken. Valuables would need to be appraised for estate tax purposes as well as for distributing or liquidating them, and different appraisers would be needed for different types of valuables. The rough estimates Ted had made after John's death as a part of inventorying Mr. Carr's assets would not be adequate for estate tax purposes. The jewelry would require an appraiser, the paintings another, the furnishings another, the rare books yet another, the silverware another, and of course the house and separate lot would need to be appraised by real estate professionals. There was also considerable repair work and upgrading that needed to be done to get the house into shape for marketing.

It was a grand house, but little maintenance had been done on it in recent years, and the upstairs area especially needed a facelift. For example, there had been a standard-sized refrigerator installed on the upstairs balcony for Mr. Carr's convenience, and it had leaked and ruined some of the carpeting.

Then there were his records and files to consider. "Earl," said Ted, "I need to go through Mr. Carr's paper records and see what needs to be saved and what can be thrown away. Can you lead me to them?"

Earl laughed. "Ted, have you ever wondered what happens to old suitcases? Well, in Mr. Carr's case, that was his filing system. He filled up his old suitcases with bills, receipts, papers of all kinds. Some of those suitcases are under beds, and the older ones are in the storage space over the garage."

Ted followed Earl from place to place, shaking his head at the magnitude of the problem. Nothing had ever been thrown away, it seemed. He determined he would start with the more recent ones. He found that, for those earlier than the three or four years that needed to be retained for tax purposes, the main problem was that the dispensable records were mixed with personal memorabilia, correspondence, and items like jewelry appraisals that had sentimental or potentially financial value - meaning that it was impossible indiscriminately to discard large batches of old documents. They would have to be reviewed much more closely. There was also an attic where old beds and mattresses, broken chairs and bagged mystery items had been stashed away.

There were massive amounts of silver, flatware, and hollowware, stored appropriately in a massive 19th Century French credenza and separate buffet sideboard, prized furniture which Ted had already decided should be sold through Sotheby's or Christie's because of their obvious high quality, rarity and value, unless someone from among the Carr heirs wished to use a part of their inheritances to purchase at their appraised value. Ted contemplated that, in the case of items not specifically designated for particular beneficiaries under the will, he would have them appraised and would allow the Carr heirs to bid on them at the appraised value or higher.

He would market items of the estate to outsiders only to the extent family members did not opt to buy them by using their inheritance money. There were estate sales specialists who would stage estate sales, and who had a list of regular customers who came to and bought at all significant estate sales. All the bids by family members would be added up and would be distributed back to them, so that they would get equal value, in cash, property or - most likely - a combination. Of course, individual items designated in the will to go to specific beneficiaries would go to them outright, with no strings attached, and without any effect on their share of the residuary estate. The rest would be mainly sold at estate sales, with the unsold residue generally donated to libraries (in the case of books) or to charities.

It was a very long process that went harmoniously in terms of Ted's relationships with the Carr heirs and their relationships with each other. After the estate sales had been conducted and the house had largely been emptied of valuables (except for some furnishings left temporarily for real estate sales staging purposes), it was time for the house itself to be marketed. A couple of the Carr family were real estate agents, Rand's wife Tammy and Zander's grandson Kimbo, and they were jointly given the sales agency rights to market the house. The sales effort was bumpier than expected, but at last the house itself was sold. The sales price was somewhat disappointing. Despite many grand features of the house, there were aspects that did not appeal to modern tastes and lifestyles.

For one thing, hardly anyone liked the location of the elevator. For another, there were only two baths for the four upstairs bedrooms and adding another bath would have been difficult to fit in architecturally. The parking on the grounds of the house was limited also, more suited to smaller cars of an earlier era, and fewer of them than in modern households where each person tends to have a car. But the family was ultimately satisfied that the house and adjacent lot sold for a fair price in the then current market.

After the sale of the house, Ted saw to the removal of all the staging furnishings. He stopped and spent a long time looking at the photographs on the wall of the upstairs overhanging balcony. He had left them in place during the sales period because they seemed both glamorous and nostalgic. They were photographs of Mr. Carr as a young man. He looked so elegant, so sophisticated, so "in charge" – and very handsome. And there were photographs of him and his wife before her much-too-early death. Ted had not known Mr. Carr at the time those photographs were made, and indeed he would have been a teenager at the time and did not even live in Greenville, but when he later met Mr. Carr, the gentleman still had the self-assured poise and elegance shown in the photographs. Ted took the photographs off the wall and would dispense them to the family members.

After paying the estate taxes and clearing the way for the settling of the estate, he called a meeting of the Carr heirs, to explain to them the process, answer questions and be sure everyone understood exactly how the final distribution would be made. This would presumably be a final meeting with the Carr heirs as his executorship drew to a close. He had worked well with all of them, including Rand, and he sensed that his relationship with Rand had become good, although they had never actually had any kind of conversation with Rand that could be described as a closure or full reconciliation.

He opened with a few remarks: "We have been through a long process together. I hope you have understood each step along the way, and I wanted to be sure you each knew what your respective monetary distributions would be, according to the data sheets already provided to you. I hope we have all come to know each other better during the time since I came into your lives. I cannot and do not fault you for having questions about this strange lawyer, whom you did not know, who turned out to be your father's designee to handle his affairs when he was unable to do so and ultimately to serve as Executor under his Will. The relationship I had with your father was a fine professional one, based on mutual respect and trust, and you ended up having that relationship thrust upon you, without your knowledge or consent. I never wanted nor expected that I would ever play the role I have been in, but it happened, and I had to see it through because I made a vow that you by now have all heard about. I have honored that vow at no small cost to myself. Yet, it has been a blessing to me in many ways. I have come to know you and count you now as my good friends, without regard to what happened during the unfortunate litigation. I want you to know that I understand your reluctance to accept me, and I hope you can understand why my commitment to your amazing Dad required me to persevere notwithstanding any opposition engendered by my involvement.

"As I have said before, I am an ordinary person, born into a loving but financially struggling family, losing both my parents while still in high school, going to Columbia and Virginia on scholarships and working for my meals. Still, I kept my faith and my values, and they have seen me through some very trying times. I hope you know that you can trust me, that I keep my commitments and play honestly with you about every detail. I assume you have reviewed the calculations I sent you regarding your inheritances, and I will try to answer any questions you might have. The figures have been checked and double-checked, and even triple-checked, but if you think there is any error, please let me know, and I will check and correct anything that might be incorrect. Whatever the monetary amounts may be that you inherit, I think they do not compare to your legacy in just having Mr. Carr as your father, and of course John Carr as your uncle. Those are the most enviable legacies of all. Money can't buy them."

No one had any questions about the inheritances. They thanked Ted. As they began to leave, Rand Carr came to him and said, "I'm sorry about the litigation, really sorry. But I wanted to ask you something. I understand you play some golf and that your group has its outings every Wednesday afternoon. Would it bother you if I joined your group?"

Ted Born understood that this was not just about golf but was about reconciliation as well. "Bother me? I'd be honored, and I am sure the whole group would be. I've heard you are a really good golfer.

"Rand, I appreciate what you just said about the litigation. Of course, it hurt when the new power of attorney surfaced, and when my name and reputation were put in issue. I couldn't understand at the time why that happened. But, looking back at it, I can see things a little better. I know you and your Uncle Jesse thought it was just wrong for an outsider to be thrust upon the family, to take charge of your Dad's care and finances, and there seemed no way to change that except by getting him to sign a new power of attorney. I would guess the reasoning was that this produced the right result even if it negated your Dad's long-time planning. And you operated under the belief I would be charging an exorbitant fee, besides. Once litigation gets started, it sometimes gets out of control. Sadly, it can just turn nasty. But I don't play the blame game or harbor negative feelings. I wish I could have been reconciled with your Uncle Jesse before his passing. I will always regret that. But I am really glad we have had a chance to speak frankly, face to face. I have sensed that, throughout the settlement process, we have come to know each other better. Although this is the first time you and I have spoken about it, I sensed that there was trust and reconciliation on your part toward me, and I want you to know that I sincerely have no ill feelings, and, indeed, nothing but the highest esteem for you. The past has passed, and it is time for a new beginning. Can we shake on that?" Rand nodded and extended his hand that was firmly grasped by Ted.

"Now, back to golf," Ted continued. "Most of us in our group are not very good, just weekly duffers. I took up the game only a couple of years ago, and I know I will never be very good. It's too late for me. I'm confident you would raise our reputation and standing. I'm excited you want to join us. I don't think it will be hard to get in but let me know if I can help. Our group also gets together for dinner one night every month, with our wives, and it would be great for you and Tammy to join us."

"Thanks, Ted. I'll see if I can work it out. Hope to see you soon on the links," replied Rand.

Ted had assumed that his reconciliation with Rand had been a gradual and unspoken process, where it was unnecessary to deal with it explicitly. He was glad Rand had taken the step to articulate the relationship status and was a bit regretful that he himself had not initiated the discussion. But it was all good that it was done.

CHAPTER TWENTY-SEVEN

EPILOGUE

Ted Born was about to leave the locker room at the gym when Greg Tween came through the door. "Hi, Greg. How's everything?" Ted greeted him.

"Everything's fine with me, still practicing law and making runs between my office and the Probate Court. How are you doing?" Greg responded.

"I'm doing well, Greg. I'm handling some cases on a selective basis, but I'm also doing some things I always wanted to do but have never had time for in the past. I've always had this fascination with 'Wonders of the World.' I had a book by that name as a child, with a lot of mostly black-and-white pictures of iconic places, and I had dreams of going to Easter Island to see the Moai, the

Great Wall of China, the Pyramids, and the Taj Mahal - places like that. In my childhood, I never thought I would ever actually see those places, but now I have had a little window of time when I could do it. I signed up for a National Geographic Trip Around the World, and I saw those things, plus a lot of others, like the Serengeti, and Angkor Wat, and Machu Pichu. I splurged for this once in a lifetime opportunity. There are still some other things I want to do, like going to Antarctica, but I might or might not be able to work that out. I highly recommend travel, that is, meaningful travel - not just travel to beaches and spas - while you are still able to do it. My mother-in-law has just had her 100th birthday, and she's okay right now, but I am sure we will need to stay nearby more and more, to make sure she gets the care she needs, and this could limit future extended travel. By the way, you might or might not have kept up with the Carr case. We closed it out a while back, and the settlement of the estate went smoothly, although it was complicated and took a lot of work. Mr. Carr was a remarkable person, and I am fortunate to have known and worked with him," Ted reported.

"I have kept up with it a little bit through Bruce and Rand Carr. I don't know a lot of details of what happened after my brief tenure in that case. Anyway, I hear you won, and I congratulate you. You know, I counseled Jesse to settle the case at the very outset. I thought the best solution would have been for you and Jesse to have joint powers of attorney and to be joint trustees and potentially joint executors, but Jesse put his foot down, wouldn't hear of that. He thought I was a softie, didn't have enough fight in me, so he replaced me, as you know," Greg reminisced.

"Yes, but you did have an important 'supporting role,' I would say, a little later on, Greg," Ted replied. "You may remember writing an email to my partner Rod Olson, essentially saying that, although you were neutral, you were passing on to Rod a conversation you had had with Mona Shadduck, in which she told you she had out-maneuvered me, outflanking me by filing a parallel lawsuit in the Circuit Court essentially making me the defendant, the villain. You said Mona believed the Circuit Court Judge seemed to be favorable to Jesse's position, and she felt the Judge would be severely punitive toward me and my law firm, and that I was going to be facing financial ruin - as well as destruction of my personal and professional reputations. I would be portrayed as a predatory lawyer spurred on by visions of big fees, to the detriment of my - as she apparently put it - 'former' client. She claimed that, if I challenged Mr. Carr's mental competency, I would be cruelly disparaging my 'former' client, breaching my fiduciary duty to him in multiple ways. I will never forget that email. It said there might be a possibility of avoiding all this inevitable financial ruin and reputation destruction if we quickly dropped the case, but we would probably have to pay damages to Jesse and Mr. Carr to do so, though possibly in 'manageable' amounts. Do you remember that email, Greg?"

"I do remember it. I apologize if it offended you, Ted. Mona was gloating and was almost ready to celebrate her victory. To me, it seemed to look bad for you and your firm. I asked Mona if she minded if I contacted you about it, and she said she did not mind. I really thought I was doing you a favor, because sometimes when a person is in the middle of a lawsuit it is easy to lose perspective and not see the handwriting on the wall. So, I just wanted you to have the benefit of an outside view on the way the case looked to me, even though it later turned out I was wrong," said Greg.

"No apologies necessary. But one thing has frankly bothered me that I want to ask you about: Why did you send the message to Rod instead of to me directly?" Ted asked.

"It was because, when I asked Mona for permission to relay the conversation I had just had with her, she asked me to send the message through Rod. She said that if I sent it directly to you, you were so hard-headed you would bury it and it would do no good. She wanted to be sure your Firm got the message. I got the feeling some of the Carr boys might have already tried to go over your head to the Firm's management, and you had resisted Firm pressure. A lot of that is speculation on my part, but I do know she wanted me to communicate through Rod. So, that's the reason, Ted. Of course, I knew you would get the message. I guess I also thought it would sound too 'preachy,' if I sent it directly to you, like I was lecturing you or threatening you if I sent it to you directly. So, maybe that also influenced my decision. Looking back, though, I realize that I did not follow proper protocol," Greg explained, taking a seat on one of the locker room benches. Ted also eased down on a bench facing Greg.

"I don't care about protocol, Greg," said Ted. "That's not important to me. Maybe I shouldn't even have brought up the subject with you, but the experience was so traumatic, at the time, that it has been a kind of wound that just will not go away. I needed closure, just to talk it out with you – no ill will, just closure, just putting the loose ends together that have remained unconnected in my mind. Just bear with me and remember that the email came at the lowest point in the case, from my point of view. I hadn't cared at all about hanging on to Mr. Carr in order to get a fee. I had lots of other clients who would pay as much as or more than I would be charging Mr. Carr. I thought about just letting Jesse take over and be done with it. Possibly I would have followed through on that if anyone - *other than Jesse* – had showed up with a new power of attorney displacing me. Yes, I probably would have just let it go. But for all those years Mr. Carr had admonished me never to let Jesse have anything to do with his financial affairs, and he had extracted a vow, an oath, from me that I would not let that happen. I could not walk away from this situation without seeking the oversight of the Probate Court, which I did by simply asking the Court for instructions as to whether I should honor the new papers. You were there for that first hearing. You heard me tell the Court that I would accept whatever decision the Court might make.

"But then," Ted continued, "the case exploded, first in the Probate Court, then in the Circuit Court. I had only asked for the Probate Court's oversight, not for any specific result, and I got vilified for that. It appeared to us the Circuit Judge was hostile, or at least unsympathetic, that the new papers, reversing 25 years of Mr. Carr's estate planning, might be the result of undue influence or, perhaps, exploitation of dementia in a 93-year-old person, who indisputably had all kinds of other infirmities. I was personally named as a defendant in the Circuit Court, blamed for dereliction of my fiduciary duties, greed, trying to hang on for money. It appeared that the Circuit Court was deliberately racing the Probate Court to trial. At the same time, I had lawyers in my own Firm urging me to drop the case, get out of it, perhaps at any price, to scurry away with my tail between my legs. Nothing seemed to be going well, and everybody seemed against me. I really did have everything on the line, my personal finances, my relationship with my Firm, my personal reputation, and my professional reputation, just as you said in your email. We work for a lifetime building up a good name, helping clients - the practice of law was always a kind of ministry to me, a way to do good - and suddenly because of just ONE crazy case where my motives were attacked, there was a real possibility, maybe a probability, that it would go up in flames, a lifetime of good works turning overnight into an irreparably smeared legacy and ruin."

"I'm sorry for my part in that, Ted. I really meant no harm. I have always had a high regard for you, and that's why I wrote that message to Rod Olson. Believe me!" Greg pleaded.

"No, you misunderstand me, Greg. It was tough for me at the time. But I now know it was a great favor, a blessing. It had a shock effect on me that I needed – one of those big life-influencing events. It caused me to take inventory of myself, who I was and what my values were. We can, I suppose, run for cover whenever there is the prospect of anything risky and dangerous on the horizon, yielding to our instinct for self-preservation. Or we can take a stand for what is right, taking necessary but dangerous risks, sometimes putting it all, and I mean everything, on the line. Sometimes life presents us with tests, and my test this time came in the darkest point in the Carr litigation. I had to face up to who Ted Born was, yes, an ordinary person, but someone tethered to values greater than himself. After much thought and meditation, I put aside the advice to run and hide, and I made the choice to do what I thought was right, risking the consequences of a possible lost cause.

"I made the decision that neither my personal nor professional reputation was worth much anyway, to say nothing of my worldly goods, if I did not take a stand to defend a 25-plus-years client's wishes and admonitions where he had earnestly counted on me. As you well know, that is a responsibility a lawyer takes on when he or she takes the oath of office as a lawyer and is admitted to the bar, to put client above self. For me, it was no longer just so many nice words about my professional duty. It was reality, and it was scary. Yet I decided I could not do otherwise than put the client first, come what may, and, as it happened, my decision was vindicated in the process, not so much a vindication of myself but a vindication of the principles I clung to. But, you know, it could have well gone the other way. Mr. Carr's deposition might have doomed me and all my values and good intentions if Jesse had ultimately succeeded in turning him against me. In addition, it was critical that we got the long-shot mandamus petition granted, that might well have been denied. I might have been a loser. Had the outcome gone the other way, I think I would have had no regrets about my decision. Was it worth it? Honestly, there were times I wondered if I had made the prudent choice, and I have wondered if the trauma might have literally shortened my life a few years. But, yes, it was worth it, and it would have been worth it had everything gone the other way. I concluded the decision was more important than its impact on me," Ted said pensively.

"Gee, Ted. You must have felt like you were headed for the guillotine, and I wasn't sensitive enough about what I was doing when I sent that message to Rod. Please forgive me," Greg earnestly pleaded.

"Greg, if forgiveness were an issue, you are more than forgiven. You might not have realized the impact of your message at the time, and that is completely understand-able. I really want to thank you for making me stop and think, and I mean it, not just saying it to be polite. You need to consider it to be a contribution you made toward achieving justice in the case. We never completely antici-pate the impact of all that we do or say, but you need have no regrets. Now, I have held you up from the workout you came to do. Forgive me for that and have a good one."

The two men rose, smiled, and shook hands. Greg headed to the fitness room, and Ted walked through the exit doors.

ABOUT THE AUTHOR

Thad Long is a versatile attorney, with decades of practice handling difficult trials and other matters for defendants and plaintiffs in a changing litigious environment. His latest novel, *The Vow: Ted Born's Last Trial*, is a sequel to his earlier novel, *The Impossible Mock Orange Trial*, that garnered 5-Star ratings from readers. In the current novel. Ted Born, attempting to fulfill his commitments to a wealthy philanthropist client, finds himself the defendant in litigation in which the client's family members seek to take over the philanthropist's financial affairs and sue Born for resisting their efforts wrongly for personal gain – threatening Born with financial ruin and destruction of his personal and professional reputation in the concluding years of Born's law practice. It is a thoughtful study of the challenge of protecting the elderly from the consequences of their own mental and physical decline. Mr. Long took his undergraduate degree from Columbia

University and his law degree from the University of Virginia where he served as Comments & Projects Editor of the *Virginia Law Review* and was tapped for Order of the Coif, the Raven Society and Omicron Delta Kappa. He has consistently been listed in *Best Lawyers in America* for approximately thirty years, recognizing him in an extraordinary nine different areas of expertise, and is an elected Life Member of the prestigious American Law Institute. He has also recently been honored with the Lifetime Achievement Award from Marquis' *Who's Who in America*. Mr. Long has written and will shortly publish memoirs of his life and career.

ABOUT THE AUTHOR